This book belongs to: Rob Castillo
If found, please call
630/865-8399

Neuro-Narrative Therapy

Neuro-Narrative Therapy

New Possibilities for Emotion-Filled Conversations

Jeffrey Zimmerman

Foreword by Karl Tomm

W. W. Norton & Company
Independent Publishers Since 1923
New York • London

Copyright © 2018 by Jeffrey Zimmerman
Foreword copyright © 2018 by Karl Tomm

All rights reserved
Printed in the United States of America
First Edition

For information about permission to reproduce selections from this book, write to
Permissions, W. W. Norton & Company, Inc., 500 Fifth Avenue, New York, NY 10110

For information about special discounts for bulk purchases, please contact
W. W. Norton Special Sales at specialsales@wwnorton.com or 800-233-4830

Manufacturing by LSC Harrisonburg
Production manager: Christine Critelli

Library of Congress Cataloging-in-Publication Data
Names: Zimmerman, Jeffrey (Jeffrey L.) author.
Title: Neuro-narrative therapy : new possibilities for emotion-filled conversations /
    Jeffrey Zimmerman; foreword by Karl Tomm.
Description: First edition. | New York : W.W. Norton & Company, [2018] |
Series: A Norton professional book | Includes bibliographical references and index.
Identifiers: LCCN 2017015371 | ISBN 9780393711370 (hardcover)
Subjects: LCSH: Narrative therapy—Methodology.
Classification: LCC RC489.S74 Z56 2018 | DDC 616.89/16563—dc23 LC record
    available at https://lccn.loc.gov/2017015371W.

W. W. Norton & Company, Inc., 500 Fifth Avenue, New York, N.Y. 10110
www.wwnorton.com

W. W. Norton & Company Ltd., 15 Carlisle Street, London W1D 3BS

1 2 3 4 5 6 7 8 9 0

This book is dedicated to my mom Rhoda, who at 87 is still sharp as a tack and as caring as ever. In another era, she would have been the therapist.

Contents

Acknowledgments

I really want to thank all of the people who are members of the team that supports the version of me you all know in everyday life, and those who supported the book-writing version of me that I frequently lost sight of and often didn't believe existed. Without your love and support and encouragement I would not have pulled it off; this is your book as well. **Specifically:**

Zemeira Singer—You saved my life, I can't thank you enough! You became my local editor, someone who provided me with structure and direction in doing this work. Your fantastic editorial comments, your wise suggestions, your vision, your writing ability, and your caring all allowed me to have a platform from which to write. Your knowledge of these ideas makes you one of the leading experts in Neuro-Narrative ideas and practices; YOU should write the follow-up book.

Bill Lax—You are the person I always turn to when I need sound, sage advice tempered by love. You've rescued me so many times. Thank you for who you are to me.

Chene Swart—Your conversation with me in the car at a TC conference was the turning point in making this a possibility...Your positivity is infectious and unparalleled in the known universe. It is I who stand on your shoulders.

D'Ann Whitehead, my life partner—Forget the book; without you I wouldn't survive period. You've supported me through the many different challenges I've faced the last few years, putting up with my moods, my meltdowns, my highs, my lows. You are ALWAYS there when I need you, willing to do whatever, all with the amazing love you show me. I am so, so lucky to have been with you all of these years.

Meg Zimmerman—You are such a beautiful person and I am so proud of you. You went out of your way to give me extra love when you knew I needed it. I look forward to YOUR future.

Stephanie Zimmerman—I so miss having you in my day-to-day life!

Larry Hammer—My long time "running mate"; thanks for bearing with me during this process!

My clients—you have taught me so so much.

My Berkeley group—you have taught me much about love and connection. You are where I first started sharing these ideas, as they were in rhythm with your evolving thinking.

My old staff and students at BAFFTA—you listened patiently and with curiosity to my strange, new, not always Narrative ideas.

All the therapists and workshop sponsors who have attended my Neuro-Narrative workshops and "demanded" I write this book: this book's for you!

I also want to thank Michael White for teaching me, inspiring me, and hanging with me (I miss you), Cheryl White, you taught me to take myself seriously; and Dan Siegel, not only for your transformational thinking, but for being the kind of person you are in the world.

Thank you Stephen Madigan for taking me back in the fold, supporting my work, and making insightful comments on the Coda.

And thank you to Norton for inviting me to write this book. Deborah Malmud, my editor, for hanging in there with me and pointing me in the right direction, and Trish Watson for helping to put this book into the English language in a clearer manner.

And last, but not least, my music friends: Eric, Juice, Walt, Brit and Joe (yes, it's finished) and all others who hang out with me and rejoice in what music brings...may the Boom Boom Room and its welcoming staff continue to be our meeting hall in life.

Foreword

by Karl Tomm

In this engaging and thought-provoking book, Jeff Zimmerman integrates Narrative Therapy and Neuroscience in a unique manner. He opens a path for thicker connectivity among physiological sensing, cognitive processing, languaging, emotioning, storying, as well as interpersonal relating in our living as human beings. He illustrates how neurologically-grounded therapeutic initiatives could enable better inter-connectedness and coherence among neurons, sensations, words, meanings, feelings, interactions, and relationships.

Neuroscience probably has a lot to offer us as therapists, yet it has been very challenging to integrate this rapidly developing body of knowledge into our psychotherapeutic practices. In this volume, Jeff begins building a bridge between the two domains of Narrative Therapy and Neuroscience. He does this not only through theoretical integration, but also through "fine tuning" the systemic coupling between a therapist and a client. He explains how the nervous system of both client and therapist become attuned in the interpersonal healing process to support "rewiring" among relevant neurons in the client's brain to stabilize more wellness. He points out how the brain itself cannot distinguish between perceived threat and actual threat. He also speculates on how the mind actively protects the brain from "toxic overload." While more work can still be done in connecting these domains, Jeff is leading us towards harnessing more and more of the embodied healing potential of the therapy relationship itself.

This book provides a major service to the Narrative community by potentially rescuing Narrative therapists from the risk of becoming

increasingly "disembodied" as they seek more and more rigor in articu-
lating a preferred "text" of persons' life stories. For some time now, I
have been concerned about how privileging the "story" of people's lives
too strongly in Narrative work can have an inadvertent negative effect
by separating persons from the bodies in which they live—and depend
on—to generate those very stories. Jeff goes some distance to rectify
this situation by connecting persons' stories with their embodiment. He
offers a plausible explanation for how implicit memories in the right
brain restrain possibilities for enduring therapeutic change if they are not
somehow brought into consciousness, narrated, and reintegrated neuro-
logically. He goes further by proposing specific initiatives that therapists
can take to bring these memories into the therapy and potentially alter
problematic neuronal patterns of activity. For instance, one tool he pro-
poses is to carefully bring forth affect-filled lived experiences as unique
"moments" for neural rewiring in the safety of a supportive relationship.
By presenting us with this orientation, Jeff opens space for a wide range
of therapeutic possibilities for Narrative therapists and makes an important contribution to new developments in the field.

I would also like to say that this is an unusually intimate and personal
book. Jeff engages the reader directly from the first sentence of the Preface
with "Thanks for getting on the bus!", and concludes at the very end with
heartfelt curiosity, asking "what you think about all of this." In between,
he repeatedly introduces relevant personal and professional experiences to illustrate the applicability of the abstract concepts he describes.
Who would have imagined an author writing about his own "Not Good
Enough" version of self being triggered by a brain state? Jeff describes
his own decentered attunement efforts, his nonconscious resonance with
clients, and his right brain coupling in the nonverbal intimacy between
himself and his clients. I read the book twice to connect sufficiently with
him; to begin to appreciate the richness of what he is trying to convey.
Since then, I have found myself automatically using some of his ideas in
some of my own clinical work. It might be helpful for prospective readers
to deliberately prepare themselves to engage actively with Jeff to get the
most out of this interesting work. Enjoy the ride!

Preface

I just opened up a different door in a different kind of way.
—Bob Dylan

Thanks for getting on the bus! This book represents the culmination of over ten years of reading, thinking, and practice. In the mid-1980s through the 1990s, I was intimately involved in the beginning stages of Narrative work, writing a book (*If Problems Talked*, Zimmerman & Dickerson, 1996) and many articles, and doing countless workshops and presentations at conferences. After this period, I decided to take a sabbatical from Narrative teaching and writing to work on my personal development and to be more available to my children. Although I did present at the first Dulwich International Narrative conference in North America in June 2002, I had stopped writing and doing workshops at that point and wouldn't present again for five years. When I did present again, it was with a group that was attempting to bring Narrative ideas into Cuba—they had me at "Do you want to go to Cuba?"

During the early 2000s, I took film and screen-writing classes, addressing my passion for movies and a desire to put my head in a completely different place. Realizing eventually that I did not want to have a career as a screenwriter, I turned my hunger for new ideas to the growing area of brain science. As I began reading and thinking and devouring these ideas, inevitably they affected my clinical practice, and I began to appreciate both the ways these new ideas dovetailed with Narrative ideas and with the ways these ideas diverged. I began to teach them to the training groups I was leading for other therapists, and then to my interns and staff at Bay Area Family Therapy Training Associates. Perhaps inevitably, I ended up back in the writing world. And here we are.

This book brings ideas and implications from Interpersonal Neurobiology and Affective Neuroscience to the ideas and practices of Narrative Therapy. I don't intend this to be an exhaustive review by any means; my focus is on what I have found especially useful to my Narrative work. Perhaps, at the end, you will be motivated to do the same: read, work, and then share. In the book I review both research and clinically oriented literature. I share my own work, what went well and what did not. In the spirit of Narrative work, I also share some of my own personal issues and developments. I have found the process of combining these ideas frustrating at times, but overall very exciting. I believe in a Narrative structure; the rest of what I do evolves from that starting point.

The underlying thread of Neuro-Narrative work is emotion, a critical theoretical distinction from Narrative work, which has traditionally used Poststructural ideas as a foundational structure. *Emotion, emotion, emotion* has become my mantra; not surprisingly, emotion is considered to be the focal organizer of brain functions. Narrative Therapists who were fortunate to work with Michael White would have noticed how he rode the emotional currents with clients, despite never discussing emotion in any theoretical perspective on Narrative work. Now, I believe that it should be a critical focus in all therapies, including Narrative ones. The book is organized such that the chapters increase in complexity with respect to understandings of emotions (i.e., are scaffolded).

I use several conceits in the book, designed to bring the ideas to life and to engage you, the reader. If creating experience to bring forth emotion is the central theme, then I feel that the process of reading this book should be no less subject to this theme than the clinical work I illustrate in it. My workshops are like that as well. I use fictionalized clients as characters to organize the chapters and provide you with an evolving view of how my theoretical and clinical principles are reflected in the work with them. Client work is revealed mostly in the form of dialogues that I compiled from my clinical notes and from my ideas about the work. These examples, although derived from actual cases in my practice, are composites—they do not represent transcripts of actual sessions, and they use fictitious names. They nonetheless exemplify approaches and dialogue I have found effective in my practice.

I capitalize *Problem*, as a nod to the way Narrative Therapy externalizes, anthropomorphizes, and generally treats Problems as their own entities in doing this work. I also use all caps when I talk about MOMENTS, given the importance of this idea to my work, my interest in making this noticeable to the reader, and to attempt to "outweigh" the Problem. You will discover that re-lived experience is the key to inviting the brain to take a wider view of what is going on. When you see an asterisk (*), this indicates that you are encountering, for the first time, a concept that I define and discuss in more depth later on. The ideas presented here build on one another in the direction of more emotional complexity, but it was impossible not to use some terms and theoretical notions before I discuss them in depth.

And, I wanted to write a book about Narrative Therapy as well as about the Neuro part. I don't know about you, but for me, having a new reading about the work helps me to re-member, or add a "member" that supports my awareness of the ideas and practices of the work, even ones I had read about before.

I am pleased you are now on this journey with me, and I hope you find the ideas in this book useful in your work and in your life. And that at least you'll enjoy the ride!

Neuro-Narrative Therapy

Chapter **1**

Toward a Neuro-
Narrative Therapy

Histories of the Present Revisited

> *Most people are prisoners, thinking only about the*
> *future or living in the past. They are not in the*
> *present, and the present is where everything begins.*
> —Carlos Santana

When I was presenting Neuro-Narrative work at a Family Therapy conference, a number of audience members said they love Narrative work
but the lack of focus on affect was extremely problematic for them. Back
in the day when I would get a comment like "Narrative work is very
cognitive," I immediately became defensive, pointing to the emphasis
on "lived experience." But I get it now. We don't talk emotions, affect,
or feelings. We don't write about them, either. And much of the time we
don't take care to make sure they are present in the room with us. My
hope is that this book will begin to remediate this state of affairs, to shift
the direction toward a more emotionally full Narrative Therapy.

How did we end up here? What can neuroscience contribute that
might provide a foundation of understanding from which we can develop
new Narrative ideas and practices? For me personally, neuroscience has
made it clear why affect needs to be privileged, and how other aspects

of the ways our brain and body work need to be addressed by Narrative Therapy. The proof is that combining Neuro and Narrative has made my work more effective, efficient, and useful to a wider variety of Problems. Furthermore, given the way our culture is evolving, ideas from neuroscience might be especially helpful at this time. For example, later you will read about the growing emphasis on the right brain in the therapy world, perhaps a response to the way our left brain appears to be exerting more influence on us in our technology-based world (see Zimmerman, 2017, for a discussion about a "right shift" in psychotherapy practices). Perhaps these developments in neuroscience and the possibilities they offer are necessary to provide us balance in our lives. Might a Neuro-Narrative Therapy contribute in a similar manner?

What Is the Decade of the Brain, and What Controversies Does It Involve?

President George H. W. Bush designated 1990–1999 as the "Decade of the Brain," to make the public aware of the benefits of brain research. It seems important to note that Allan Schore (2012) marked the actual decade as 1995–2005. Despite all the attention and fanfare, initiatives derived from brain research have not been without their critics. Nikolas Rose and Joelle Abi-Rached, for example, cautioned against a "neuromolecular gaze" (2013, p. 38). They questioned the claims made by various authors (although they shockingly did not refer to Dan Siegel's work) that through this lens human beings "will know better how to achieve social and political goals" (p. 162). These authors traced the history of modern neuroscience back to 1962 and traced the prefix *neuro* to its first use in the late seventeenth century, with *neurons* being described in the late nineteenth century. The story goes that Freud wanted to situate his ideas in the developing brain science of his day, but this idea was rejected by dominant scientific ideology.

Michael White once said that there were no enmeshed families until the 1970s, a tongue-in-cheek suggestion that not until then did this description of a particular kind of family organization develop and gain use in describing families. Once brought forth, this view had real effects on the way we looked at families and was embedded in normative judgments about how families should be. At the time, was *enmeshed families* a useful construction? To what extent are, for example, neurons and synapses* useful constructs? What are the real effects of these constructs? How did the question of "real effects" even come about?

In a 2007 *Family Process* article, Mona Fishbane brought many neurobiological concepts into the Family Therapy literature including (as she described them): the relational brain, the way neurons wire together when fire together, neuroplasticity, amygdala hijacking the way our cortex has evolved for social behavior and communication, unconscious emotional operating systems, mirror neurons, mindsight, attunement, and the chemical mediation of connection. She ended her article by suggesting "that we increase our focus on clients' emotional experience, given the clear importance of emotional life emerging from neuroscience" (2007, p. 410). Has this call been met or even responded to by Narrative or Family Therapies?

In my opinion, not really. But it is important to understand why not. Like all forms of psychotherapy, Narrative Therapy arrived at a particular point both in the evolution of ideas informing psychotherapeutic work and in terms of what was happening in the larger culture.

What Contributed to the Evolution From Emotional Focus to Meaning Focus?

In the early 1980s, most soon-to-be Narrative Therapists were Family Therapists, reading and publishing in Family Therapy journals. Most of the early Family Therapy leaders had a background in Psychoanalysis and tended to think of family problems from that lens (Beels, 2009). In his 2009 *Family Process* article, Chris Beels pointed out that the influence of Psychoanalysis was to encourage the development of theories of family function and dysfunction. These theories are structural: they hypothesize various ways to understand how families worked. One effect of structural points of view is that they construct categories of "normal" and assign pathology to families that do not fit the normative structure. Nevertheless, very few of the early Family Therapists focused on emotion in their work. Indeed, Matthew Suarez Pace and Jonathan Sandberg suggested that, "traditionally, emotion has played a marginal role in the theoretical, empirical, and clinical aspects of MFT [Marriage and Family Therapy]" (2012, p. 4). They suggested that the only prominent founding Family Therapists to be emotionally focused were Murray Bowen and Virginia Satir.

In the larger therapeutic world, Psychoanalytical and Psychodynamic therapies were one of the dominant groups, with a focus that included unconscious processes and emotions. Even then, some of us critiqued their practice, suggesting that these feelings were elusive, that they sometimes required expert help to uncover, and we wondered if talking about them resulted in much change anyway. In general, in these approaches the therapist was constructed as being someone who knew more about what creates the clients experience than the client did; this was especially true with anything deemed "unconscious." The complicated issue of nonconscious influences (I prefer this term to unconscious, as do many writers today) is addressed later in the book. In retrospect, at the very least, these seemed to be unhelpful metaphors to describe clinical work.

A very different dominant trend, particularly in American psychological work, was Behaviorism. Over time thoughts came to the forefront, with the idea that these thoughts produced feelings. Eventually, the cognitive movement supplanted Behaviorism as the dominant psychological paradigm. Jerome Bruner (1986, 1990), whose ideas were central to Michael White's early work, focused on the kind of meaning-making processes that people engaged in when responding to life events.

How Did the Evolution of the Cybernetic/Systems Model Change the Question From How Families Work to What Are the Real Effects of Our Work?

White situated his early work in Gregory Bateson's ideas about restraints (Madigan, 2011) and published a paper on externalizing that referred to these ideas (White, 1988/89). Bateson was considered a founding father of Family Systems Theory whose family work can be traced back to the 1950s and whose 1972 book *Steps to an Ecology of Mind* discussed the application of cybernetics to human systems. White's reading of this work led him away from Family Systems Theory and toward a different application of some of these ideas.

Family Systems Theories and therapies based on them tended to focus on communication, structural relationships, and homeostasis, leading to ways of interacting with families that bypassed the system's "resistance" to trigger a change process. In terms of the larger context of the therapy world, Family Therapists challenged many of the ideas and practices of the dominant therapeutic ideologies, rejecting the idea of individual pathology and the idea that therapy had to be an individually focused practice. At the time, the idea of family pathology instead of individual pathology was considered revolutionary.

Cybernetics was originally tied to the image of the machine and physics, but by the late 1970s "new" or "second-order" cybernetics emerged, a model more closely resembling organisms and biology. Heinz von Foerster attributed the origin of second-order cybernetics to the attempts of classical cyberneticians to construct a model of the mind. He stated they determined that

> a brain is required to write a theory of a brain. From this follows that a theory of the brain, that has any aspirations for completeness, has to account for the writing of this theory. And even more fascinating, the writer of this theory has to account for her or himself. Translated into the domain of cybernetics, the cybernetician, by entering his own domain, has to account for his or her own activity. (quoted in Dammbeck, 2003, n.p.)

The development toward observer-dependent viewpoints mirrored developments in the larger cultural world, where Modern became Postmodern and Structural became Poststructural.

Those of us in the Family Therapy world began considering the implications of the idea that theories were observer dependent, that what was seen depended on who were doing the looking and when they looked. We began to acknowledge that the various ways we looked at families were products of the imaginations of therapists, teachers, and theorists and had little to do with how clients viewed their own lives. We embraced social-constructionist viewpoints (Gergen, 1985) and began to wonder what the world actually looked like through our clients' constructions and not just our own. We moved to maps of Problem construction and solutions, instead of maps of people and families. We began privileging client narratives and not our own. But the emotional component of these narratives was not emphasized, at least not in the way the work was described. Suarez Pace and Sandberg (2012) suggested that in the mid-1980s the only voices for considering the role of emotions in the Family Therapy literature were those of John Gottman (Gottman & Levenson, 1986) and Sue Johnson and Leslie Greenberg (Greenberg & Johnson, 1986; Johnson & Greenberg, 1987).

We read about Radical Constructivism (Watzlawick, 1984), where all reality is considered relative to someone's point of view, but Michael White (personal communication, 1991), speaking from the position of Poststructuralism, suggested this point of view goes too far because it does not take into account the real effects of the view itself. Indeed, this mantra became a lynchpin of Narrative Therapy. It wasn't that anything goes but that everything, every view, every action, had to be accountable to its real effects, including our fields' various ways of looking at families, clients, and Problems. If we view all therapeutic thinking as constructed by observers (us), then the central question becomes the real effects of these constructions.

How Did Narrative Therapy Continue the Direction of Emphasizing Meaning Making?

With encouragement from David Epston and Cheryl White, Michael White decided to take up Bruner's text analogy as a useful clinical metaphor for his work. And thus Narrative Therapy was born. Michael White used Bruner's work to suggest that we are multistoried, that we have dominant and subordinate stories we could step into, and that the dominant stories we live by leave out contradicting lived experiences. The implication was that, by inviting meaning to these unstoried experiences, they could be used in the service of alternative stories that fit clients' preferences for their lives and have good (i.e., desired) effects. These unstoried experiences were referred to as Unique Outcomes, as they could not be predicted given the Problem story.

Bruner suggested that events are linked through sequences in time and in plot; if so, questions could be generated that would bring forth and link events in this manner to form the structure of an alternative story. Again, according to Bruner, stories have a dual landscape: one of action containing events and another of meaning, containing reflections on these events. In Narrative Therapy, alternative stories begin to be mapped out along these landscapes and co-constructed between therapist and client. We are curious about clients' experiences and the meaning they give to those experiences. This process involves the therapist asking questions to create a context in which new meaning is made, with a client's personal experiences forming the substance of the New Story. It follows that, if we are going to privilege the client's knowledge and experience and not our own, then adopting a decentered position in the room is very useful in the work.

The Narrative metaphor also allows us to make the Problem not one of a damaged identity and a lack of capability but a story that doesn't fit one's preferences. This is important because it was seen as a departure from the pathologizing models of the day and countered the dominant idea that Problems were located inside people. Indeed, Problem experiences themselves were thought to reflect the effects of dominant cultural specifications; the specifications that supported these Problems could be brought forth and then deconstructed for the client.

Why Are Narrative Therapists Suspicious of Scientific Knowledge?

Narrative Therapists believe that their therapy was the first (and still only) therapy to make issues of politics and power fundamental to the work. How did that come about?

In terms of the larger culture, many of the original group of Narrative Therapists became adults in the 1970s and had personally experienced the oppressive effects of the dominant culture, which had marginalized those of us who didn't fit into what was then considered "normal." Many of us protested this marginalization, in various manners. We were feminists, antiwar protesters, civil rights workers, and proponents of alternative sexual identities. Personally, with my bohemian aunt, I passed out leaflets for CORE (Congress for Racial Equality) and, with my brothers, ate meals in her big bed (much to my parent's chagrin).

It was inevitable, perhaps, that we were suspicious of the science that gave truth status to certain dominant cultural practices and ideologies. Psychology, for example, was born to create testing procedures that would identify and weed out the "not-normals" from our cultural institutions. An interesting example of this ideology was the championing of the idea of self-actualization, which posited a hierarchy of needs specified by scientific knowledge. However, the development of the highest levels of actualization were available only to the privileged; the opportunity to reach one's "potential" was available to only 1 percent of the population. Furthermore, based on the widely accepted idea that there was a singular self, there was also the not so implicit suggestion that some selves lacked the capacity to be successfully actualized. It's no wonder that Michael White situated his work in nonpsychological bodies of thought, such as Literary Theory and Cultural Anthropology.

Narrative Therapists saw what we did as political, an effort to remediate the oppressive effects of the dominant culture in general, and scientific knowledge specifically. We adopted the rallying cry of the feminist movement, "The personal is political." By challenging the oppressive ideologies of the times, Narrative Therapy was a response to the social context it grew up in. This made Michel Foucault's (1977, 1980) work on marginalized identities a good fit to our personal experience and politics; indeed his thinking influenced much of the early ideas in Narrative Therapy. Foucault, a Poststructuralist, was interested in how marginalization, based on gender, race, social class, and sexual preferences, created categories of normal and not-normal and we thought about how this contributed to Problems. Michael White used to suggest that there were two kinds of Problems, those that evolved from clients' efforts to embrace normative functioning when it didn't fit them, and those where clients chose to embrace their nonnormative preferences and felt the punishing voice of the dominant culture in response.

Poststructuralism suggests that we operate based on pre-understandings, and that these pre-understandings are derived from cultural discourse and shape the meaning we give to experience. Foucault suggested that certain scientific discourses being held by those in positions of power and influence were being used in a way that marginalized some by creating pathological identities for those individuals. If alive today, Foucault might agree with Rose and Abi-Rached (2013) about the dangers of knowing oneself or being known through scientific neuroknowledge; in Narrative terms, seeing oneself or others through this (or any particular) lens might be referred to as a thin description. For Foucault, knowledge was power—the power to lay truth claims on how one is or should be. According to him, these truth claims led to practices such as objectification, where people are turned into subjects and scientifically classified (turning people into anorexics and schizophrenics), and subjectification, where we turn ourselves into subjects and evaluate where we do and don't fit in with the ways specified by the dominant culture. Foucault suggested that subjectification was a modern form of power, where we actually operate on ourselves, as opposed to being operated on by some external powerful other. In either case, objectification and subjectification led to the creation of unhelpful identities for ourselves and for those who wanted our help.

From my point of view today, however, Poststructural ideas have both good and not-so-good effects. These ideas did help by taking us away from models of how things "were" (models of people and practice) and pointing us instead toward models of change—how to create change became not necessarily related to the specifics of the person or family. Also, these ideas helped take us away from models of how individuals/couples/families were supposed to be (dominant specifications) and toward a focus on valuing our clients' personal preferences. One critique of Poststructuralism, however, is that the language of the work is anti-experiential. For example, *discourse* as a word or a concept is no more accessible than many words gleaned from the fields of scientific study. Furthermore, externally locating meaning in discourses took us further away from bodily based experience* and from emotion. In this way, Poststructural ideas are only half the story (Zimmerman, 2017); they help us understand the context of meaning in which emotional responses unfold.

What Distinctions Might Be Made Between Internalizing and Externalizing Discourses?

Michael White believed that the usual effect of internalizing Problems was to create Problem identities; adding a label from the *Diagnostic and Statistical Manual* gave these identities an appearance of scientific "truth." Externalizing Problems, by talking about them as separate from the person, became a practice to counter the internalization, because it separated the person from these scientifically constructed Problem identities. Externalization helped move us away from ascribing Problem meanings to the client's self and instead assign these meanings to the Problem. Externalizing the Problem also created space for clients to notice alternative aspects of themselves and their lives that had disappeared into the shadows of the Problem; these became entry points into more preferred narratives, ones that had valued effects. In contrast, internalizing Problems left clients feeling that there was something fundamentally wrong with them, that they lacked the capability to handle life's demands, often due to deficits created early in life. These kinds of formulations left us bristling at the way mothers were blamed for creating these Problems.

Michael Guilfoyle brought forth an interesting, less discussed distinction from Foucault's (1982) work, the notion of internalization. Guilfoyle suggested that "internalization refers to the application of culturally available discourse to oneself" (2009, p. 21). It is this internalized discourse that Narrative Therapists are so fond of externalizing, because these discourses support Problems and Problem-encouraged experiences of the self. Guilfoyle suggested that individuals, in an active process of engaging with the world, apply this internalized discourse to the world around them, unknowingly affecting their view of others (and for clients this includes their therapists). In effect we are "externalizing" these discourses, bringing them out of the realm of internally held truths about ourselves. These now externalized discourses influence persons' evaluations of others based on their accommodation (or not) to the demands of these once internalized discourses. If individuals and their relationships can be unknowingly influenced by this discursive process, it raises the question for me about what other influences might be unknowingly operating.

What about internal experiences as opposed to internalized ones? Where does internalized experience sit in the body? Does internalized discourse trigger body based reactions like emotions? Or, more likely, is the process of internalizing actually set into motion by a triggering of strong affect? There seems to be no question in Narrative work that becoming aware of and naming these internalized discourses is an important part of externalizing and situating Problems; in this book I discuss how doing so relates to bringing forth internal experiences as well. Externalization is liberating for us and for clients, although it does lead to some complications that were invisible to us back in the day, such as creating confusion by externalizing the internalized discourse but leaving internal experience in the body.

What Kind of Therapeutic Work Might Be a Response to Today's Social Context?

All eras have psychotherapies that emerged as a reflection of the current cultural context (e.g., Psychoanalysis at the turn of the twentieth century, Behaviorism in the 1920s and 1930s, Humanistic Psychology in the 1960s, Poststructuralism in the 1980s). In the twenty-first century, while way too many people still live without privilege and entitlement, many of those who fill psychotherapy practices bring with them Problems that reflect their participation in an entitled, electronic world. They require psychotherapies consonant with the issues of the day. What are the real effects of understanding today's psychotherapeutic endeavors through a lens that has not evolved to take into account today's world? To return to Narrative Therapy's interest in addressing oppression, who and what are oppressed in Western culture today? Our right brains, which are dominated by the effects of technology (see Chapter 5)? As in previous generations, some of my millennial clients experience either a sense of not living up to dominant cultural specifications or a feeling that the cultural specifications do not fit them. Yet, this generation in general appears to have a more entitled and less oppressed position toward relationships and institutions of power. Indeed, my younger clients (whom I love and who are terrific with me) tell me that what they notice as Problems for themselves and their peers is selfishness/overentitlement and a lack of loyalty and persistence (e.g., a tendency to jump from one thing to the next quickly by leaving the old behind and starting anew). More importantly, they are concerned about a thinning connection to people in general and to larger groups, but a greater connection to electronic devices (often through which they relate to others). As do any set of generational knowledges and practices, these have real effects, some of which contribute to Problems as they operate today. What kind of counterpractices might help address these types of Problems, and how might these constitute the psychotherapies of today? How might the psychotherapeutic ideas that are emerging reflect what is needed in today's world?

I think it's time for some brain science.

Chapter 2

Possibilities in Neuro-Narrative Therapy

Preview and Backstory

> *My brain, it's my second favorite organ.*
> —Woody Allen

Neuro or Narrative: what's your guess on the following quotes?

"By directing our attention, we can go from being influenced by factors within and around us, to influencing them . . . but we don't have to allow them to bully us or define us." (2011, p. 102)

"Psychotherapy can be seen as a deep, transformational form of collaboration. Our clients are our colleagues: we are companions along the journey together." (2010a, p. 149)

"Yet our patients are also experts in their own right, deeply knowledgeable in other domains. Our patients are certainly expert in being themselves." (2010a, p. 56)

"Ultimately we as clinicians are companions along the road of life with our patients. Trust emerges when we realize that the false separation created by the cloak of professional identity is just an illusion. Each of us, therapist and client alike, is doing the best we can." (2010a, p.87) "I can freely say that my patients have changed me. I am who I am because of them." (2010a, p. 55)

And commenting on the field of mental health:

"What is going on in the field that this focus on disorder is so prevalent? Why isn't the field called 'mental dysfunction'?" (2012b, p. 38-4)

Narrative Therapists might imagine one of our own saying these things (maybe without using the term *patient*). Surprisingly, these are all quotes from Dan Siegel. Here's one from a client of his: "Amazing realization: I can feel this change . . . my thoughts and feelings come up, sometimes big, sometimes bad . . . but they used to feel like who I was and now they're becoming more like an experience I'm having, not who I am, they don't define who I am" (2010b, p. 96). Here's an interesting comment on brains and social construction from Joseph LeDoux's book *Synaptic Self* (2002):

> One much discussed distinction is between the minimum and the narrative self. The former is an immediate conscious-ness of one's self, and the latter a coherent self-consciousness that extends with past and future stories that we tell about ourselves. The narrative self bears some relation to the post-modern notion that the self is socially constructed. While social construction is often viewed as diametrically opposed to scientific view of man, the two are not necessarily at odds with each other since brains, in the end, are responsible for both the behaviors that collectively constitute the social milieu, and for the reception by each individual of the infor-mation conveyed by this milieu. (p. 20)

Based on the Heinz von Foerster's quote in Chapter 1 regarding second-order cybernetics, that "a brain is required to write a theory of a brain," it would appear he would agree.

Interpersonal Neurobiology Backstory

It's important to realize that brain science is not a therapeutic theory but a set of ideas that can be useful to all therapists. One important idea in Interpersonal Neurobiology (IPNB) is integration, which involves differentiating systems (in this book's case, Neuro and Narrative) and then linking them together (which I am attempting to do with these ideas). From an IPNB perspective, integration leads to the ability to respond more flexibly, allowing for decision-making based on preferences. Personally, I have gone through multiple versions of myself as a therapist, related to how my life has evolved both professionally and personally. What I learned through this process is that therapeutic ideas can be combined in multiple ways, but it is important to adhere to a consistent overriding metastructure. I believe that integration is consistent with Narrative ideas and practices, especially if we consider that we are attempting to integrate our clients' lives with their personal preferences.

Perhaps of interest to those who have worked in systems models, Siegel conceptualizes the brain as an open system, even suggesting that a larger system is created through the linking to other brains. (Family Systems Therapists view families as open systems as well.) Open systems take in influences from the outside (i.e., the environment) and are also open to change from within the system. Siegel suggested that any complex system has "a 'self organizing' property that emerges in the interaction of elements of the system" (2012a, p. 28). Change occurs via increasing integration through differentiating various parts and then linking them together, increasing the system's ability to adapt to changing circumstances. In this manner, the brain (or family) maintains stability while allowing for possibilities of change. Nevertheless, some brains get rigid and inflexible or become chaotic (as do families from this point of view). In these situations, integration has failed to occur, or parts have become dis-integrated.

Some Brain Basics

As background for approaching a Neuro-Narrative perspective, let's consider some basic aspects of our brains: when and why different parts of it evolved, and the important role of neurons and synapses.

The Triune Brain

One way to look at the brain is to consider when different parts of it evolved, called the Triune Brain: the "reptilian" brainstem/cerebellum, the "mammalian" amygdala/limbic system, and the "modern" neocortex.

The "reptilian" part of our brain evolved about 300 million years ago and operates on instinctual reactions that mediate survival and control the body's vital functions, such as heart rate, breathing, and body temperature. Our human brainstems and cerebellums, which mediate these instinctual reactions, are about same size as a gorilla's.

The "mammalian brain," which evolved approximately 200 million years ago, generates safety appraisals through the amygdala and the distributed limbic areas. Generating responses through this newer system took us away from reacting purely on instinct; the mammalian emotional system has thus evolved to allow for much more complexity and choice. In contrast to the reptilian part, the human limbic areas are twice as big as a gorilla's.

The neocortex, which fully formed 100,000 years ago, mediates more complex thinking and motor activities, as well as speech and language. About 250,000 years ago, during the Ice Age, this area of the brain evolved to handle new environmental demands (such as communication for the purpose of working together to store food); later it further evolved to take on more subtle demands, such as managing emotions to facilitate living with others. We humans have a neocortex three times as big as a gorilla's. The prefrontal cortex links the three "brains" to one another and helps modulate the input from the lower areas of the brain.

Neurons and Synapses

We have about 100 billion neurons in our brains. These neurons use electrical conduction and only unipolar (one-directional) firing. Neurons fire up to a few hundred times a second in the neocortex, only a few times a second in the limbic area, and only with the right environmental triggers in the reptilian part of the brain.

In the late 1800s, Freud proclaimed neurons to be the substance of psychological processes. This turned out to be incorrect—we now know that synapses are the building blocks of psychological processes. We have about 1,000–10,000 synapses per neuron. Synapses use chemical conduction: charges are sent down the neuron, and when enough charge accumulates, it activates a chemical response, which changes the charge of the cell from negative to positive and releases neurotransmitters into the synapse, which excite or inhibit the other neurons connected by the synapse.

Novelty strongly triggers a synaptic response, as does focused attention. For example, one theory about attention-deficit disorder is that not enough norepinephrine (which excites) is released, resulting in too little cortical arousal. This permits subcortical emotional systems to govern behavior instead, resulting in reactivity and impulsivity. As you might suspect, stimulants activate norepinephrine.

Probably the best-known tag-line from brain science is a summary statement of Donald Hebb's (1949) ideas: Neurons that fire together, wire together. Once connected through synapses, neural networks are formed that govern a range of responses, such as mood, behavior, and states of mind*.

The Name Is Not the Thing!

Around 1995 I presented Narrative ideas to the veteran Family Therapy faculty at the Mental Research Institute in Palo Alto. When I discussed the importance of attending specifically to gender issues, Paul Watzlawick turned to me and said, "I am reminded of a quote from Gregory Bateson: 'The name is not the thing.'" Watzlawick was questioning the value of privileging any predetermined construction. Happily, I had my wits about me and acknowledged that, while gender was a construction, it was an important one that had real effects on all of us (I was aware that the women were all sitting to one side and weren't speaking). The women in the room very quietly agreed. From a brain science perspective, not only is the name not the thing, but also the thing is not the thing—it's only a mental representation of the thing. In a sense, the "thing" is a story, as the mind* re-presents what is out there in a form that is influenced by experience.

As all signals, external or internal, require neural translation, what happens in the brain during these activities involves the creation of *neural maps*: clusters of neurons that fire in a pattern that symbolizes a neural representation of various things. These maps then shape how we perceive future similar experiences. Along with a neural process, we have a mental one, a subjective experience; within this experience we believe that what we are seeing or how we are understanding things are true and not dependent on prior experience or neural translation. In other words, as suggested by Bateson (1972), the map is not the territory, just a take on it, a neural version. We are constantly reconstructing mental experiences and co-constructing them with others.

Once again, there are Poststructural objections to deconstructing ourselves around neural lines. Nikolas Rose and Joelle Abi-Rached suggested that "dethroning the self-possessed self and its illusions of reality by culture and language is one thing, and dethroning the perceptual capacities of the self-possessed self by the non-conscious, automatic, evolutionary shaped functioning of neurons and their hard-and-soft-wired interconnections is quite another" (2013, p. 209). I suspect that, given a distrust of science and a love of Poststructuralism, this could represent the feelings of some veteran Narrative Therapists. Ironically, as just described, neural translation is required to interpret the experience of culture (see the quote above from LeDoux); all translations are done in the brain and by the mind, by neurons and their interconnections.

Narrative, IPNB Style

Siegel stated that, "for at least 40,000 years we have been making sense of our world by bringing the inside out" (2012a, p. 383) and "that stories are created within a social context between human minds" (p. 370). This suggests that, by telling stories to others, we use our relationships to make sense of what we are thinking and feeling. Narrative Therapy has always suggested that dominant stories account for what we remember and how we remember it; if we create stories in this social manner, then these remembrances, these stories, are relationally shaped. Siegel went on to suggest that even how we learn to put words together in a story form is derived from our early relational experiences. Seemingly echoing Jerome Bruner's landscapes of action and consciousness, Siegel stated that the contents of these stories are our human lives and mental experiences.

What happens when narratives are full of the details of life but aren't full of "mental experiences"? Siegel (2012a) suggested that narratives require both left- and right-hemisphere modes of processing*. While the left hemisphere's drive to understand cause-and-effect relationships (landscape of action) is the primary motivation of the narrative process, coherent narratives require both the interpreting left hemisphere *and* the right hemisphere's collection of what is going on in our mind, for example, our feelings, desires, beliefs, and purposes (landscape of consciousness). Margaret Wilkinson referred to Jaak Panksepp's comment that left-hemisphere story lines become "more superficial and disconnected from the deep affective needs and life-stories of people" when there is damage to the right hemisphere (2010, p. 41), and also noted Panksepp's suggestion that, without right-hemisphere involvement, the left "becomes more adept at self-serving rationalizations" (p. 42). Wilkinson stated, "Experience processed in the right hemisphere becomes the determinant of the narrative that is developed into its final form in the left" (p. 126).

What happens when the two are not well linked? Certain life experiences can have the effect of blocking access to the internal awareness of one's emotions and bodily sensations. One effect of this dis-integration would be that these individuals' stories are dominated by the nonmentalizing representations of the left hemisphere. In turn, holding these "thin" narratives has real effects not only on themselves but also on their interpersonal interactions. Later in the book I review my work with my client Doug, which will demonstrate what this lack of integration looks like, what the effects are, and how I used this understanding to help him develop more fully formed narratives.

Addressing the makeup of narratives, Wilkinson noted that "narratives highlight smells, colors and emotions associated with the experience" (2010, p. 124). These are right-brain functions. Inviting these kinds of details while listening to client stories facilitates a story reconstruction that engages the right brain. These kinds of details are also critical in bringing back the important affect-filled memories that might trigger new narratives. Along these same lines, Wilkinson noted that the right brain is dominant for novelty and is likely oriented to deviations from the expected. Might Unique Outcomes, when coupled with emotional arousal, more powerfully steal the attention away from the Problem through their novel information?

Autobiographical memories are located in the right hemisphere. Processing emotional words activates the right hemisphere (Schore, 2012), allowing access to the autobiographical memories needed for constructing narratives that are not limited by the left brain's cause-and-effect approach. In Narrative Therapy, thickening alternative stories by inviting strong emotion-filled descriptions thereby affects the storying process by opening it up to the full range of material from one's life. In contrast, Problem-supporting narratives are often sustained by the absence of critical information characteristics of the left brain's utilitarian approach. These narratives become, as Panksepp suggested, empty explanations of why the Problem is correct. In Narrative language, these are *very* thin descriptions.

In general, storytelling is a way we make sense to ourselves of our overall life experience. The events of the day are combined with memories of previous experiences under the influence of established themes in a specific relational context. As we are inevitably influenced by listeners' expectations, when and to whom we tell stories have real effects on their flavor. Besides the overall implications of this for the therapy process, Narrative Therapy re-membering questions are good examples of inviting a story that is shaped by the images of preferred others and by the telling of this story in the context of a therapeutic relationship.

From a developmental standpoint, when parents engage in reflective dialogue with their children, this provides experience in the co-construction of narratives. Siegel suggested that these dyads enter into a form of bilateral resonance; their left brains are interacting verbally, while their right brains are registering their nonverbal communications, their "shared emotion," which Alan Sroufe noted is the fabric of social relationships (as cited in Siegel, 2012a, p. 375). This description appears to mirror the process of what can happen in therapy. Indeed, Wilkinson (2010) suggested that when affect is brought forth and regulated in a secure relationship, a new coherent narrative emerges that is tied more to the present than to the past. Chapter 5 returns to the discussion of factors that facilitate the development of new narratives.

An interesting distinction can be made between coherent and cohesive stories. Siegel defines *coherence* as having a quality of emergence, a conceptual and nonconceptual sense of knowing. These stories are open and fluid. From clients we might get Problem stories that are *cohesive*: well put together by their left brains but with a flat, rigid, lifeless sense about them. As implied, storying without emotion isn't meaningful. To bring some life to these cohesive but not coherent Problem stories, they must be connected more directly to the emotional systems that are largely influential in generating them.

In summary, the narrative function in the brain is to give meaning to experience, but as you will see throughout this book, to be meaning-full, we need to invite the participation of both hemispheres. Bringing in the more emotional right brain more fully into conversations allows them to be both affective and effective.

Introduction to Possibilities

When people hear the term *Narrative Therapy*, they often imagine it is merely about telling stories. While we do want to invite storytelling, many of the ideas and practices of Narrative Therapy use the guidance of a Narrative metaphor. Besides the aforementioned influence of Jerome Bruner (dual landscapes of action and consciousness, text analogy), Michael White's and David Epston's early work also reflected the influences of Victor Turner (1969; rites of passage), Barbara Myerhoff (1982; definitional ceremony/outsider witness groups), and Clifford Geertz (1973; thin and thick descriptions). Geertz wrote that "the drive to make sense out of experience, to give it form and order, is evidently as real and pressing as the more familiar biological needs" (1973, p. 140). He was also interested in the role of symbols in creating meaning. Interestingly, these authors' ideas can be readily translated into IPNB concepts. For example, symbols (Geertz) bring forth right-brain processes; I use them with my client Doug to help integrate emotions into his stories. Bringing forth the stories of our lives in a relational context (i.e., creating narratives) is the essence of Myerhoff's work and central to the idea of outsider witness groups. In addition, turning a thin description (the Problems version) into a thicker one (the more preferred story) involves inviting more experience into the New Story, resulting in a more extensive neural network to make it more influential. During the thickening process, the Problem networks will continue to have influence along with the developing alternative network, reflecting the betwixt and between nature of the change process (illustrated by Turner's rites-of-passage metaphor); at different times old and new both affect responses.

It is important to note that these Possibilities and their content are not meant to be inclusive of all of the work in neurobiology or affective neuroscience. In many respects, they are more like areas of study; my intention is to invite your curiosity into the connections between these areas of study and Narrative Therapy, in hopes that you will further pursue what interests you.

Possibilities 1. The Importance of Affect: The Emotional Side Has Not Been Discussed in Narrative Therapy

For therapy to be effective, affect must be brought forth, but in the Narrative Therapy literature emotions have rarely been mentioned descriptively or theoretically. To be clear, *emotions* refers to the hardwired systems in our brains; *affect* is the outward reflection of these emotions, and *feelings* refers to our subjective experience. In the literature, *affect* is the term that is used as a general reference point.

Classic narrative practices can bring forth a lot of emotion, but this does not inevitably occur. If you have been lucky enough to witness Michael White at work, either in person or on video, you will have noticed how masterfully he was able to zero in on what was most emotionally salient for the client, reflecting the client's affect (sometimes with tears in his eyes or a broad smile full of joy on his face). His work was far from being emotionless, despite removing the language of emotions from his inquiries into clients' lives. Historically, the point of not addressing the concept of emotions was to do away with privileging the therapist's supposed expert knowledge about the client's *unconscious* (nonconscious) drives and emotions. As I have mentioned before, this was a political act in its time. We believed it was important to put the client's language and experience front and center. Perhaps unintentionally, the effect of moving in this direction led to affect being left by the wayside in the Narrative literature and (sometimes) in practice. But the idea was never to get rid of emotion altogether.

From the standpoints of IPNB and Affective Neuroscience, the implications for privileging emotions are quite clear and are at the heart of all therapeutic work. LeDoux (2002) presented a diagram showing how "talk therapy" (insight, instruction, problem solving, musing) is mediated in the part of the prefrontal cortex that has a circuitous connection to the amygdala (part of the distributed limbic system), while conversations that involve emotional arousal instead light up the part of the prefrontal cortex that has a direct connection to the limbic region. The amygdala/limbic area mediates all the bad, uncomfortable affect that supports Problems. Narrative Therapy conversations that are not grounded emotionally are no different from other talk therapies. Sometimes emotionally connected conversations occur spontaneously, without any extra effort or attention, but many times they do not. The degree to which this happens depends on how integrated emotions are into the client's conversation (which reflect their overall integration in the client's experience), as well as on the therapist's level of comfort and attunement to emotions (both the therapist's and the client's).

I had a client who would do most of what he needed to do to be successful in his work life and then would stop just short of finishing the process. No amount of standard Narrative work seemed to make a difference. When we explored his experience of the death of his mother when he was a teenager, this made a difference. Exploring didn't mean discussing it or looking at its effects; instead, we were able to bring forth the stored implicit affect* related to his painful experiences with his mom. Here you can see how emotions have meaning too; once he was able to reexperience the affect associated with her death (with me there to listen and help him through it), he was able to make a connection between this and the meaning "success" had for him. Our therapeutic process allowed for a re-membered relationship with his mother that separated out her death from the goals he had for his life.

One of the consequences of explicitly privileging meaning and implicitly avoiding emotion has been that we often accept responses from clients that are logical or rhetorical but not embodied. Without *embodiment*, without recalling the emotional state, we are unable to actually restory the painful or difficult experience. This means that while the New Story remains intellectually compelling, the more emotional Problem story remains privileged. It continues to feel like the true story because, from a neural perspective, it is. I have also found that when I don't attend to my client's affect, one effect is that the client shares rhetorical positions rather than lived emotion-filled experience.

With the goal of making certain that emotions are integrated into the practice of Narrative Therapy, Chapter 3 we will look at (a) the seven emotional systems in the brain and their critical role in our functioning; (b) using moments of experience as an important aspect of the interviewing process; and (c) the critical role of affect in both internalizing discourse and the process of deconstructing its effects.

Possibilities 2. Body/Mindfulness: This One Is Personal!

Meditation changed my life, no question about it. Despite living in California since 1988, meditation always seemed a little new agey to me. I couldn't imagine how it would have such helpful effects. Through my reading in brain science, particularly Siegel's books, I discovered that brain scientists were all very enthusiastic about meditation. Perhaps the compelling data that meditating for three months for just twelve minutes a day results in measurable changes in the brain (Lazar et al., 2005) contributed to this enthusiasm. I read *The Mindful Therapist* (Siegel, 2010a) and began doing the meditation practices in the book. At first it was difficult, and I complained to my friends who meditated that it made things worse. They laughed and said that I was noticing my mind's buzz more. I protested, but shortly I discovered that they were correct. Turns out the data were right; I can't say for certain that it changed my brain, but I can say my mind began to work differently.

What were the real effects of meditation for me? After starting to meditate, I noticed that my relationship to myself as well as to others in my life had changed. I became much more open to people and kinder to them and to myself. I found myself generally being (and often without much effort) more decentered in relation to others, seeing their separate experience and mine more clearly. I experienced more feeling in my body and even felt the Problem more in my body during therapeutic conversations. I could clear my head of chitter-chatter by noticing it and breathing it out. And I'm less reactive to things in general; for example, I don't yell in my car anymore in response to traffic and drivers—not most of the time, anyway. My overall resting level of stress is lower, and I now have a tool for handling stressful situations when they occur. Indeed, meditation facilitated a process that allowed me to take on the Problem that for a while was interfering with writing this book. The combination of meditation and Narrative practices is a pretty potent one. You will see examples of this work later in the book.

In general, meditation contributes to an almost natural externalization of what is in your mind—while meditating I can imagine things in my life as separate from myself. Once separate, I have more space to respond to things from a position of choice instead of just reacting to them. An interesting example of this involves me more easily noticing that I am participating in my own subjectification, as mindfulness makes it easier for me to notice the way dominant discourse is compelling me. Once I notice this, because I am able to be in a position of greater choice, my preferred responses become easier to use. This is not surprising, as meditation seems to engage the prefrontal cortex and helps develop integrative fibers between it and the reactive amygdala.

Now I even think it is actually unethical not to recommend meditation to clients. I know that's a pretty controversial statement—really controversial for Narrative Therapists, as recommending means centering my knowledge with respect to the clients, a Narrative no-no (although I bet there's not one among you that some of the time doesn't make some kind of sometimes useful recommendation to clients). Meditation is that helpful, efficient, and effective.

In Chapter 4, Siegel's definition of *mind* and its relationship to the brain is discussed. You will see that Poststructural pre-understandings, the influence of cultural discourse, is part of what contributes to the top-down influences* that make up the mind. In addition to how our personal experience contributes to how our minds work, we can add our species' entire cultural history to these top-down influences. Co-construction of meaning involves two minds, both client's and therapist's, and both are subject to top-down influences. Finally, I address the critical area of bodies and bodywork, underdeveloped in Narrative

Therapy—separating the person from the Problem doesn't have to mean separating the person from their body.

Possibilities 3. Right-Brain to Right-Brain Communication: The Therapeutic Relationship Is a Rich Resource

We are hardwired to take in relational signals and connect with others; this is biologically important for survival. Through our mirror neuron system, we take in social experience, which allows us to detect others' intentions and internal states. Indeed, we register messages from others at a speed that makes these messages unavailable to conscious processing. This is a right-brain to right-brain communication process, and it is the dominant mode with which we connect to others. As 60 percent of communication is nonverbal, it seems that the focus in psychotherapy on left-brain verbal meaning making has left out a lot of what the right brain has to offer; it is here that relational communication is transmitted. One implication is that psychotherapy may actually be more of a right-brain to right-brain affair.

The left brain (landscape of action) uses a strategy of arriving at a dominant story that fits the situation but, as previously suggested, does not take into account all of the information (despite leaving us believing the story is true). Bringing in the right brain, where the landscape of consciousness and identity resides, is critical to being able to dislodge what Siegel referred to as the stubborn left. Furthermore, given the technological direction our culture is taking, promoting right-brain activity might prove to be a psychotherapeutic must.

Perhaps all this means that we should consider beginning to consciously use input from both our hemispheres in our co-constructions with clients. Specifically, I am suggesting that taking in and responding to nonverbal "relationship communications" might be useful and important. Ironically, also for historical reasons, despite Narrative Therapy considering itself a relational therapy, the relationship between therapist and client was considered off-limits as a topic of conversation. In Chapter 5 I advocate for "process issues" to be part of the Narrative Therapy conversation. I review ideas that suggest that affective, moment-to-moment relational experience is the most critical factor in creating new meaning. Questions that address this level of experience in relation to the Problem could possibly make a huge contribution to our work. I believe that something that happens between people creates narrative change.

Possibilities 4. Nonconscious Influences: Affect Has a Past That Influences Identities

This will be the most controversial area of discussion for Narrative Therapists, who have, again for historical reasons, long eschewed anything nonconscious in favor of conscious purpose.

As I stated, Narrative Therapy has never embraced the notion of an individual self. Instead, we have privileged the idea of multiple versions of the self or multiple identities, and it turns out that multiplicity is clearly the case as far as brain science is concerned. Neural networks evolve from experience to form states of mind*, and we have an infinite number of these states. Some have more influence than others, and the effects of some are certainly more preferred than others; what makes it hard to hold on to the preferred states is addressed in Chapter 6.

Memory is a subject much discussed in the trauma literature. We know that all experience is encoded; this includes both the experiences that contribute to the Problem and those that stand outside the Problem story. How much influence any of these experiences has is a different question. We will spend quite some time understanding the body's and mind's response to stress and how memories contribute to that response, particularly the influence of stored implicit affects. It turns out that the brain doesn't differentiate between internal threats (i.e., stressful stored affect) and external threats. In other words, handling and managing difficult feelings from the past is no different to the brain than being confronted with, say, a velociraptor. As long as these stored, stressful affects remain unstoried, they can have a strong influence that can override carefully constructed alternative stories.

I also describe how human connection shapes neural connection. Parents and caretakers of young humans happen to make up the infants' early environment and are preprogrammed to lend their right brains to these developing minds. Babies' brains are born underdeveloped and require assistance from another brain both to facilitate the development of right-brain neural structures and for the purpose of self-regulation*. One effect of this developmental process is that the child learns a model for recognizing and managing dangerous situations (both internal and external ones). This model may have different effects in different contexts; one effect may lead to false positives, where danger is predicted when there is none.

Let's now begin our journey by turning to the subject of affect.

Chapter 3

The Importance of Affect in Narrative Therapy

There is a crack in everything that you can put together: physical objects, mental objects, constructions of any kind. But that's where the light gets in . . .
—Leonard Cohen

Matt, a twenty-eight-year-old white, heterosexual project manager, consulted me on some Problems that were interfering with his dating relationships:

J: Tell me about the Problem or Problems that have been hanging around you.

M: All my dating relationships end the same way. We date, I quickly decide that I'm not ready to be more involved, and then I unilaterally end the relationship because I find reasons not to trust them. I've actually been dating my present girlfriend for a year, but now I intensely feel she's not to be trusted.

J: How does this Lack of Trust affect you?

M: It brings up loads of Insecurities.

J: And how do these Insecurities give you a hard time?

M: I obsess about her going out with friends, and this comes out in

me picking fights with her. Afterward I am embarrassed. But then
I text with her about this to get her to prove her love.

J: I'd like to come back to that . . . but I was curious about what
effects these Insecurities are having on your relationship.

M: I tell her that the relationship is over . . .

*There was a bit of an angry tone from Matt in the above conversation,
but I was struck with what I imagined was hurt, despite him sharing most of
what he said in a reporting tone of voice. Why not ask about these feelings
directly? My fantasy is that he would have said, "Sure I'm hurt," but in a
matter-of-fact way, without the hurt really being embodied in his conversation. Instead, I believed it would be useful to create the conditions in which
the hurt would enter his body directly. Without these feelings being directly
present, the conversation is really thin.*

Of course, it is not news that emotions are relevant to psychotherapeutic
work. We all know that feelings matter. But how exactly do we work
with them in therapy? Do we explicitly address them? If so, how does
this create change? Narrative Therapy has never explicitly addressed the
issue of emotions or involved them in its conceptualization of how therapy changes people's lives. This chapter discusses the role that emotions
play, why this is important, and how it fits in with how Narrative work
has traditionally been done.

Classic Narrative Therapy Practices and Considerations

A Narrative Therapy session often begins by inviting clients to share
their experience of the Problems that are influencing their lives. Problems are generally spoken about using externalizing language, in order
to separate the Problem from the clients' identity and to open space for
them to notice aspects of their lives not taken over by the Problem:

J: Tell me about the Problem or Problems that have been hanging
around you.

M: All my dating relationships end the same way. We date, I quickly

decide that I'm not ready to be more involved, and then I unilater-
ally end the relationship because I find reasons not to trust them.
I've actually been dating my present girlfriend for a year, but now
I intensely feel she's not to be trusted.

The externalizing process is then extended by asking questions about
the real effects of the Problem, which has the additional benefit of getting clients to begin to notice, in a new way, what the Problem is doing
to their life:

J: How does this Lack of Trust affect you?
M: It brings up loads of Insecurities.

Externalizations are fluid. They are meant to be useful ways to represent
the client's experience but do not represent any one truth about what the
Problem is. They evolve during the course of the work. Before integrating
"Neuro" into Narrative work, I privileged externalizations that reflected
self stories, or identity conclusions. I believe that these internalized versions of the self are shaped by dominant cultural beliefs and thus stand
in the way of people enacting their preferred stories. Usually, conclusions in these stories reflect perceived shortcomings, such as Not Good
Enough, Inadequate (a common theme for men), or Lack of Entitlement
(a common theme for women). These conclusions represent inevitable
ways individuals fall short of the dominant cultural specifications for
their gender or social location. Because these self stories tend to be influential in most territories of people's lives, externalizing them facilitates
mapping out the Problem's broad influence, which is useful both for
noticing the Problem's effects and for finding areas of resistance to the
Problem. With this in mind I might have asked, How do these Insecurities affect your view of yourself?

Although I still believe that these identity conclusions are important
in the way I described, I didn't go there with Matt because I am currently
more interested in getting at the affect fueling these conclusions. So I
stayed with Insecurities for the time being, as this construction offered
a lot of arenas in which the Problem was influential and more clearly
opened the door for an affective component. As I am always interested in

the strategies Problems use to influence people, I framed the next question in a way that brought these strategies forward:

> J: And how do these Insecurities give you a hard time?
> M: I obsess about her going out with friends, and this comes out in me picking fights with her. Afterward I am embarrassed. But then I text with her about this to get her to prove her love.

The way Matt said "prove her love" made me imagine that he knows his girlfriend loves him but the Insecurities are preventing him from being confident in that knowledge. I filed away his preferred understanding, planning to return to it. I did not address it at this time, as I believed he needed to share more about his experience of the Problem and needed to feel understood by me. As in most therapies, there is a relational aspect to this work, a process issue that is critical to the outcome. I also felt that proceeding with mapping out the influence of the Problem on him and on other aspects of his life (e.g., on his relationship, his girlfriend, his work, and on his other relationships) would be useful at this point:

> J: I'd like to come back to that . . . but I was curious about what effects these Insecurities are having on your relationship.
> M: I tell her that the relationship is over . . .

I was able to invite out the meaning he was giving to his experience, but reading the dialogue it is difficult to tell that, despite whatever words he used, the affect behind them was not present, either in the room or in his body, as he spoke—perhaps this was too uncomfortable for him? Stored implicit affect can feel quite dangerous. Congruence between his words and his tone of voice, facial expression, body posture, and how I am feeling in my body all contributed to my feeling that something was missing in the conversation.

A typical Narrative Therapy process might involve continuing to ask questions about effects, and effects of effects. These questions might then evolve toward deconstruction of dominant cultural specifications, bringing forward the "pre-understandings," the texts that these specifications draw upon. In the case of white, upper-middle-class, straight individuals, these questions might be about gender. Asking Matt's opinion about these effects might follow:

What are the effects on your girlfriend and on the relationship when the Problem gets you to tell her the relationship is over?

What do you imagine it might be like for a woman, when a man unilaterally decides the relationship is over?

What do you think about the Problem doing this to you, and getting you to do that to her?

If clients do take a stand against the Problem, clearly noticing the effects of it in a new way, and stating their new found dislike of it, it is often useful to invite them to justify their evaluation of the Problem:

You say that you think it's wrong for Insecurities to get you to say things that are hurtful to her . . . why do you think it's wrong?

What values do you hold that Insecurities are taking you away from when you are being hurtful to her in this way?

We hope that the effects of these kinds of questions allow clients greater access to the values they hold that stand against the Problem. This is an example of Michael White's metaphor of scaffolding, an idea he got from Lev Vygotsky (1978) and Jerome Bruner. Scaffolding involves continuing to ask questions that distance the person further and further from the Problem. One kind of question that reliably distances the person from the Problem involves collapsing time on the direction the Problem is taking them:

If Insecurities continue to get you to break up with her over and over again, what will things be like in, say, six months?

An interesting thing about this question is that it seems to invite the client to very strongly feel the danger involved in continuing to be influenced by the Problem. Bringing forth fear in relation to cooperating with the Problem stands in sharp contrast to the way the Problem has been making the client feel: that it is dangerous to resist the Problem.

Often during externalizing conversations (which can occur over one or a number of sessions), clients spontaneously offer examples of times when they did otherwise than what the Problem suggests. Originally called Unique Outcomes in the Narrative literature, these become entry points into alternative stories. One helpful way to get a picture of what might represent a Unique Outcome would be to imagine extending the Problem's sphere of influence over as much of a person's life as possible and then noticing where the Problem is not having any influence (later I describe an example of this with Matt). These Problem-free areas can be noticed with the client and labeled as anti-Problem developments as they represent areas of resistance to the Problem. Interviewing the client about them involves the therapist engaging in similar categories of questions as with the Problem. For example, asking about the effects of these anti-Problem developments (these may be actions, thoughts, or feelings) helps the client notice more clearly what difference these areas of resistance have made to their lives. Like with the Problem, evaluating these effects and situating them in the client's value system begins to make them more meaningful. Narrative Therapists have long been interested in understanding developments as examples of resistance. Michel Foucault suggested that there was always resistance to dominant cultural specifications. These developments often reflect the client's preferences that stand outside these specifications. Indeed, from a Narrative Therapy perspective, Problems themselves can often be understood as reflecting a client's protest against these specifications (later I show how this might be true for Matt).

Once a New Story has been constructed, it needs to be further thickened and given additional support. Bringing forth valued past relationships is a start:

"Who would have been least surprised to see you take these steps?"

Inviting clients to "catch up" important people in their lives on these new directions can occur via letters or even invitations to come to a session. In Narrative work, these re-membering practices are designed to give relational support to new stories. Interestingly, this kind of relational thinking is entirely consistent with ideas from Interpersonal Neurobiology (IPNB).

Finally, like with Problems, collapsing time on the direction the New Story might take the client is useful and will bring forth a possible outcome to the New Story that feels good and safe:

> If these new directions take hold of your life, what might things be like for you in six months? A year? Five years?

Here is my version of the traditional Statement of Position map (White, 2007) for addressing both Problems and developments. This is a generic map that is useful for inviting clients to take a position against the Problem (as opposed to continuing to justify their cooperation with it, the stance they often are taking when they start therapy). Once a position is taken and developments noticed, then these development questions further the construction of New Stories:

Problem	Developments
Externalizing problems	Unique Outcomes
Effects	Effects
Deconstruction	Resistance to specifications
Evaluation	Evaluation—preferred?
Justification	Justification—with past relationships
Scaffold	Circulation of New Story
Collapse time	Future

We will soon take a look at a Neuro-Narrative–influenced version of this map.

One more clinical piece before turning our attention to emotion and how privileging affect might influence our work. This example from Dan Siegel's (2010b, p. 247) work with Sandy, a twelve-year-old girl who had developed Fears, and rituals to deal with these Fears, nicely encapsulates what I believe is useful in a process of externalization, the move from affect (i.e., terror) to externalization (the checker):

> We started to do role-plays around different scenarios. Suppose she was having lunch in her neighbor's backyard and the checker got activated. What would it say?
>
> **Checker:** Don't get too close to the edge of the pool. They might jump out and grab you.
>
> **Sandy:** Thank you checker for your love and concern. I know you want to keep me safe, and I want to be safe, too. But your enthusiasm is too much, and it's not necessary to keep me safe.

This kind of dialogue is in sharp contrast to the internal battle that often takes place before treatment. "I can't believe how stupid I am—what an idiot!" If you have a fight with yourself, who can win?

If she could identify and label the checker at work and recognize that the checker has its own drives and needs, she could begin to differentiate it from the sheer terror she'd been experiencing.

Why Is Affect So Important From a Brain Science Perspective?

Since 2005, bringing affect more consciously and directly into Narrative work has been the focus of my teaching. I have also discussed this at length in two articles (Beaudoin & Zimmerman, 2011; Zimmerman & Beaudoin, 2015) and addressed this as part of a bigger picture in a third article (Zimmerman, 2017). Narrative Therapy, despite focusing on experience and meaning, has not included bodily based emotional meanings as part of its descriptions of its practice. "Experience" has ended up lacking the affective flavor that it needs. Indeed, it could seem that we had a case of split brains: our left brains were talking to clients' left brains, without a conscious focus on what was going on between our right brains. I believe that despite White modeling affective involvement, his concerns about situating Narrative theory in affective terms contributed to this state of affairs. A whole generation of Narrative Therapists, learning primarily from White's *Maps of Narrative Practice* (2007), may have ended up with an overly cognitive picture, missing the "spirit" of the work (S. Madigan, personal communication, 2014). I also believe that those of us who have taught this work, despite being invested in working with experience and creating experiences for trainees, were not focusing specifically on the affective aspects of what we were doing.

When I read some of the literature on emotional systems, it became compelling to me why emotions should be privileged in our work. Jaak Panksepp (1998, 2009, 2012), who has done extensive work on emotional systems, suggested that the brain is a deeply affective organ with a variety of evolved feeling states that guide living. Emotional systems are the underlying operating system—the ROM space, if you will. In contrast, our cortex is programmed by experience (our software) and is meant to be secondary to the main operating system. To illustrate this point, Panksepp suggested that you can remove the cortex from an animal and it can function—in fact, all instinctual expressions such as basic emotions remain intact. But the opposite is not true: damage to the emotional/limbic areas of the brain is more devastating than damage to the cognitive-neocortical areas. Affective mentality is meant to have more influence over us than our cognitive functions.

Emotions are evolution's way of giving vital information: Is what's going on around us good for survival or not? Is this something we need to pay attention to or do something about? Richard Davidson and Sharon Begley suggested that emotions are "facilitating" (2012, p. 89). Emotions are a source of energy; if the emotions are negative they are usually energy consuming, involving fast reaction times and avoidance-oriented behaviors (except for anger, which is approach-oriented). An area of the brain called the right insula mediates negative emotions. Rick Hanson (2013) suggested that the faster reaction times of negative emotions, and the presence of a lot more words for them than for positive emotions, reflect our brain's wiring for survival and contributes to our flight-fight response; according to Hanson, this allows us eat lunch rather than be lunch. Strong negative emotions also amplify our stress response, requiring us to manage this bodily based arousal (this is critical to discussions in Chapter 6). If the emotions are positive, they are approach-oriented and enrich energy. They are mediated by our left insula, and they likely evolved because of the need to live with others.

How do these emotional systems work? Basic emotions can be aroused from subcortical brain regions by activating neurochemical circuits. An external stimulus leads to an appraisal that activates a bodily based response, a physical state of arousal that cues an emotional experience. These emotional systems assess the extent to which goals are being met in the external environment and reset us to meet these circumstances. In effect, it is emotions that focus us, not thoughts. Furthermore, emotions did not evolve as conscious feelings. Bodily based emotional experiences precede and shape our felt emotional responses. Introception, the ability to read our own body state, is also modulated by the insula, where we become aware of our felt response. Some of us have had experiences in life that have led our minds to dampen the flow of energy and information* from our insula to our bodies, the effect being that we are less aware of our moment-to-moment felt experience. Nevertheless, whether aware of these feelings or not, they can still be quite influential. Developing awareness of what is happening inside of us makes it easier to learn to manage these difficult feelings; the practice of externalization, either as a part of therapy or through meditation practices, helps bring forth, contain, manage, and regulate negative emotions.

Neurobiologists coined the phrase "To name it is to tame it," with the caveat that the feeling or response can be effectively tamed only if it is accurately named. Interestingly, those who meditate consistently are able to name emotional responses influencing them more accurately than those who do not. This finding implies that increased awareness of emotions is a critical first step to naming and externalizing and therefore managing Problems. Lynne Angus and Leslie Greenberg (2011) cited research suggesting that accepting one's negative emotions (which means feeling them first) actually decreases and protects against depression.

Emotional Systems in the Brain:
Our Chemical Lives

Panksepp's model suggests that the brain is guided by seven emotional systems: SEEKING, FEAR, RAGE, PANIC/GRIEF, LUST, CARE, and PLAY. What kind of emotional system do you imagine gets activated when my client Matt fears a loss of his primary special connection? How might this emotional system fuel his responses? My hope is that spending time reviewing these systems will serve as an example of the chemical aspects of our emotional lives and illustrate how important emotional systems are to our functioning.

> M: I obsess about her going out with friends, and this comes out in me picking fights with her. Afterward I am embarrassed. But then I text with her about this to get her to prove her love.

Time to panic? According to Panksepp, the PANIC/GRIEF system is located in the same area of the brain where our pain response system is located; rejection feels a lot like physical pain. Believe it or not, taking Tylenol makes you feel better in either case. It might surprise you to learn that this system is actually separate from the FEAR system. Separation distress can invite anticipatory anxiety (FEAR system), but not vice versa; anticipatory anxiety and panic attacks are generated by distinct neural systems. Different drugs help one but not the other: benzodiazepines help with fear; antidepressants help with panic attacks and separation distress. Interestingly, people who experience panic attacks often have a history of childhood separation anxiety. My client Matt, for example, had many significant experiences that led him to have an extrasensitized PANIC system.

Panksepp (1998) presented an interesting chart that compares the symptoms of separation distress and of opiate withdrawal. These include psychic pain, crying, loss of appetite, depression, and sleeplessness. Why might this be so? When we interact with someone we know, endogenous opioids are released in the brain, increasing the likelihood that those individuals will be sought out again. In contrast, the loss of someone very close to us results in losing these natural brain opioids, leading to withdrawal effects. People who are satiated with opioids bond less; if lacking in social interaction, they need more opioids. Not surprisingly, the histories of drug addicts are filled with separation, loss, and lack of connection. Opiate addiction, then, can be thought of as pharmacologically induced positive feelings of connectedness, an experience that others derive from social interaction. From this point of view, addiction both leads to and is an effect of social isolation.

The CARE system adds to our understanding of what might be happening with Matt and provides a good example of the differences that occur by gender. Oxytocin, usually more abundant in female brains, leads females to tend and befriend, to be calm and connect. It is no wonder men experience more health benefits from marriage than do women. While this chemical is present in the brains of both genders, females have more of it. When males ejaculate, oxytocin is released, leading to more proximity and nurturant responding from them. Animals prefer to spend time with other animals with which they have experienced high brain oxytocin and opioid activity, that is, family and friends, than with strangers. Is texting the modern-day format for decreasing separation distress and triggering these connecting chemicals? I wonder what effects this will have over time on how this system operates, as text interactions do not occur face to face, and facial cues are thought to be critical to attachment processes.

Recall that through texting and other means, Matt pursued his girlfriend; our SEEKING system generates motivation for exploration, particularly in relationship to survival needs (food, water, warmth, and sex). Furthermore, when it is late in our workday and those Narrative questions aren't popping out, and we don't feel as curious, it is likely that our SEEKING system is depleted. As we all know, stimulants (chemical retriggering) get the SEEKING system reactivated, and the questions come back. All this makes me wonder if asking the kinds of questions that invite curiosity from our clients activates their SEEKING system. In addition, does the process of Narrative Therapy mobilize the clients' SEEKING system by helping them notice that the Problem is blocking, through its effects, access to important desired resources? If so, arousing the emotions related to the loss of sex (LUST) or connection (PANIC/ GRIEF) might be very useful.

As I will show, Matt, and many other men in his position, react very strongly to the presence of other males in their girlfriends' lives. One aspect of the RAGE system is inter-male competition, fueled by testosterone. Female hyenas, which have a lot of testosterone, show more of this competitive behavior with one another than do females of other species; testosterone is also high in pregnant females and, of course, in men. In today's world, competitive victory comes in many forms, such as graduating high in your class from a prestigious school or going into a highly valued profession. These accomplishments actually increase the secretion of testosterone, which in turn reinforces future assertive behavior. Flaunting these accomplishments represents dominance displays, which are not necessarily aggressive but instead are mating invitations to females. Panksepp noted that females are hardwired to pay attention to and want to mate with assertive males, as these behaviors are seen as having survival value (maybe that's why women are more interested in rock stars than therapists). A Poststructural perspective relates bullying to male entitlement and culturally sanctioned aggression, but when Matt vents his rage on his girlfriend it is in line with what Panksepp suggested happens when complex creatures vent their rage on more submissive animals and avoid confronting more dominant ones.

The PLAY system is more active in the morning and involves rough-and-tumble play. As children have different developmental trajectories, imagine the effects for kids in school whose PLAY system is still very active and yet their behavior must conform to classroom structure? Problem-dominated conclusions about their identity seem inevitable. Furthermore, despite evidence that increased physical play reduces attention deficit disorders, Ritalin is frequently used instead; this drug has the effect of reducing PLAY system firing and thus interfering with the important influence of this system. When Matt (and so many other men) "playfully" teases his partner, does this reflect an attempt to invite contact in a form that conforms with dominant specifications for men? It is my experience that, while men experience teasing as playful, women experience it as hurtful and aggressive and would much prefer to get a hug.

As far as the LUST system goes, we can imagine what might happen when the SEEKING system is encouraging pursuit of sex and yet the RAGE system is blocking it from being sought within a distressed couple's relationship. In this situation, how much does the SEEKING system encourage men to look outside the marriage, and how much of men's behavior is influenced by entitlement? In cultures where women's entitlement has increased, it does appear that their LUST system has led them to the same behaviors as men (increased affairs). Indeed, in this Millennial era, cultural specifications have evolved to make "hooking up" (i.e., having multiple, short-lasting sexual partners) a dominant practice for young people; these changes in social/sexual behavior are great examples of the way our emotional systems coevolve with dominant social specifications to produce behaviors specific to different eras. In the Narrative Therapy world, we have traditionally viewed these developments from a Poststructural lens (see Zimmerman, 2017), but adding the effects of hardwired emotional systems helps round out the picture. If you are interested, I suggest you check out Panksepp's book *The Archaeology of Mind: Neuroevolutionary Origins of Human Emotions* (2012) for a much more in-depth review of the implications of these systems.

The big point for us is the extent to which these hardwired, biochemically transacted emotional systems motivate and shape our thinking and behavior. The forms this thinking and behavior take are shaped by our social environment and can continue to be shaped by experience throughout our lifetime. Nevertheless, these chemically mediated systems have as much to do with social behavior as do socially specified ways of acting—it's not just discourse. Here are some further conclusions:

Emotional processes provide natural internal values, and these values arise from bodily processes and neural events.

Our emotional systems operate independent of consciousness and thus involve implicit learning.*

Experience is shaped by subcortical affective reactions, with cortically supplied meanings that are influenced by dominant cultural discourse.

Problems are thus supported by negative affect and the conclusions/meanings that are encouraged.

The location of Problems is therefore both in the emotional systems in

the body and in the discourses, but not at all in our identities, person-
alities, or capabilities.

For example, the Insecurities plaguing Matt began as overwhelming
affect, a firing of his emotional systems. This firing was influenced by his
personal experiences. To account for this emotional arousal, his mind
produced a story about what was happening. This story was of course
influenced by dominant cultural discourse and included conclusions
about his girlfriend and himself. Ultimately, these experiences with his
girlfriend contributed to an ongoing story about Matt's lack of value as a
person. While dominant discourse attempts to define what constitutes
value for any of us, it is emotional arousal that sets the storying process
in motion.

Emotions, Arousal, and Story

What about the FEAR system? We all know what it feels like when our
FEAR system is activated—apprehensive tension, sweating, and an accel-
erated heartbeat are just some of its effects. This system often gets activated
in humans in response to dark places, high places, approaching strangers
(especially with angry faces), sudden sounds, snakes, and spiders. These
fears are hardwired, as opposed to being learned through experience.
When our FEAR system is activated, we usually experience the desire to
escape or avoid these situations; interestingly, we experience the same
desire to flee in situations when past personal experiences have led to us
perceiving danger, as our brain actually cannot distinguish between actual
threat and perceived threat. The FEAR system can also suppress the other
emotional systems, interfering with their functioning. Classic examples of
this include how Fear can create discomfort when seeking what one wants
(e.g., sex, desired accomplishments) and can interfere with expressing rage
and with accepting care (many interpersonal problems are the result of
Fear being triggered alongside connection). In this manner, these effects
contribute to some of the Problems our clients experience.

Activation of the FEAR system proves to be a particular challenge to
psychotherapy because we are hardwired for negative affect to impact

us more powerfully than cognition or positive affect. The connections going from the fear-generating amygdala to our cortex are thicker and denser than the ones going from the cortex to the amygdala (neurons are unipolar and go in only one direction), with the effect that negative affect is generated faster and more intensely than our cognitive responses—it is simply not a fair fight for cognition. (For other discussions of the effects of this neural arrangement, see Zimmerman & Beaudoin, 2015; Beaudoin & Zimmerman, 2011.) In addition, as suggested previously, engaging in "cognitive" conversations (insight, instruction, musing, or problem solving) does not directly address the Problem (Fear) as the area of our brains that is involved in these types of conversations is only indirectly connected to our emotional systems. When our conversations do not activate our emotional systems directly, it takes a lot more work for therapy to begin to influence the emotional responses that mediate problem behavior.

Imagine what happens when Matt discovers his girlfriend texting with her ex-boyfriend. Neuroception is the continuous monitoring by our brain of our external and internal environments for danger signs (Porges, 2004). This ongoing appraisal of danger is influenced by our history of experiences with events of a similar type; these experiences dictate whether Fear gets triggered. Danger triggers may be genetically programmed (e.g., snakes), or they may be learned. The survival value of this process seems obvious, yet what we learn to respond to as dangerous may fall in the category of false positives—we may see danger where there is none. This kind of experiential learning provides the foundation for the Problem that takes over Matt, as he is constantly reading danger into things his girlfriend does despite her assurances to the contrary. Later, we will see that this danger involves not only what his girlfriend might do (external threat) but also how it would make him feel inside if she did it (internal threat).

When a Problem is triggered as a result of this danger response, it affects perception, long-term memory, attention, and working memory. This accounts for the difficulties clients often have remembering these experiences, or their having remembrances different from those of others that were involved. Our social and self-engagement systems are shut down, which is why we want to isolate from others when Problems are around. Flight, fight, or freeze is the order of the moment, not thinking; it puts us in a reactive, nonreceptive state. You might even notice your client reacting this way during a consultation, perhaps even to you. When this triggering occurs, in our prefrontal cortex we come up with an explanation to account for what we are experiencing emotionally. To repeat, *emotional reactions influence stories more than the other way around*; meaning is shaped by this limbic arousal (i.e., is it good or bad? do you approach or avoid?). Let's take a look at how this works.

According to Siegel (2012a), emotions are a flow of energy, a state of arousal and activation, flowing through the brain and other parts of the body. He suggested that when information enters the brain via sensory systems, the representations generated from the perceptual processes are eventually passed on to the amygdala, where they are appraised and given initial value. This initial orientation comes with a sensation of "pay attention now." Next, as the value systems of the brain continue to appraise the meaning, we might experience sensations like "this is good" or "this is bad." An appraisal of "good" might come with activation of the SEEKING system—it makes us curious and want to investigate more; "bad" might bring on activation of FEAR, PANIC, or RAGE, depending on the context. What we call a person's affect is the outward reflection of what they may be experiencing inside, with the caveat that some have learned to automatically dampen this emotional flow to the extent that there is no external reflection. In any case, it is only after this appraisal process that these emotional reactions become what we experience as feelings. Siegel went on to suggest that the primary emotions generated in this process are the beginning of how the mind creates meaning, and that emotion and meaning are generated by the activation of the emotional systems we have been discussing.

In Narrative Therapy, we speak about the meaning one gives to experience. I believe it is important to understand that the tone of that meaning (i.e., good, bad) is first generated by a bodily based response. This tone, this bodily based response, then both influences the interpretation of these experiences and affects which experiences are selected for storying. This view is in contrast to the Narrative Therapy idea that it is the story that selects out and interprets experiences. Simply put, *we have a feeling and then make up a story to account for it*, not the other way around.

Emotional arousal affects the way experiences of life are expressed. Siegel posited that the arousal process of emotions leads to an increased likelihood of future retrieval (i.e., memory, discussed in more detail in Chapter 6), in addition to appraisal and creation of meaning, suggesting that emotional arousal is crucial to creating new, long-lasting meaning, and thus to creating change in therapy. Matt was aroused when interacting with his girlfriend but was not easily aroused when he shared his story with me, making our conversations less likely to be meaningful. To deal with this particular challenge, which I found myself facing frequently with clients, I came up with a slightly different way of languageing some key aspects of Narrative work. I refer to the times where I bring forth affect-filled lived experiences as MOMENTS.

Problem MOMENTS

Problem MOMENTS are actual times when the Problem is influencing the person. Entering into these MOMENTS with clients is different from having them describe what happens when the Problem is around. Instead, the client is asked to pick a time when the Problem has had the effect they were concerned about, and go through this experience in detail, reexperiencing the MOMENT all the way. Let's return to Matt for an example. Here's a review of the start of my session with Matt:

J: Tell me about the Problem or Problems that have been hanging around you.

M: All my dating relationships end the same way. We date, I quickly decide that I'm not ready to be more involved, and then I unilaterally end the relationship because I find reasons not to trust them. I've actually been dating my present girlfriend for a year, but now I intensely feel she's not to be trusted.

J: How does this Lack of Trust affect you?

M: It brings up loads of Insecurities.

J: And how do these Insecurities give you a hard time?

M: I obsess about her going out with friends, and this comes out in me picking fights with her. Afterward I am embarrassed. But then I text with her about this to get her to prove her love.

J: I'd like to come back to that . . . but I was curious about what effects these Insecurities are having on your relationship.

M: I tell her that the relationship is over . . .

Here's where the conversation went next:

J: How do the Insecurities get you to do that?

M: Well, there is the issue of her texting with her ex.

J: Can you take me through the moment the last time that happened?

M: Sure . . . I walked into my kitchen, saw her phone sitting there, and picked it up. I noticed there was a text from her ex-boyfriend. I began to imagine her going back to him . . . (his voice became raised as he continued) I told her to call me when she was "really" broken up.

J: Can you picture the moment when Insecurities got you imagining that? What was going on in your body?

M: I was thinking about the pain of her breaking up with me.

J: That pain must be really hard to deal with . . . Why do you think the Insecurities want you to imagine that?

Inviting Matt to enter into a Problem MOMENT shifted the direction of the conversation. He went from reporting on his experience to sharing an affect-filled experience with me in the session. Among the effects of this shift were his feeling the Problem in a new way (further inviting Insecurities to be the Problem instead of his girlfriend) and his experiencing and sharing these feelings in the context of a relationship (in this case with me). This allowed me to make an attuned response to him (notice that in the last response above I first acknowledged his pain before asking my next question). Asking the MOMENT question also allowed me to thicken the emotional experi-ence in his body. Inviting Matt to consider why the Insecurities wanted him to "imagine that" was intended to further separate him from the Problem by getting him to notice the Problem's motives and begin to experience negative affect toward the Problem itself.

"Tell me a story" is a refrain I have used in my teaching to help students stay focused on eliciting their clients' experiences. How is this different from MOMENTS? MOMENTS bring forth a story in a particular way, one that facilitates the clients reexperiencing what has occurred. Entering into these lived MOMENTS with my clients has the effect of bringing emotional arousal into their bodies and into our relationship. In Narrative Therapy, we speak about descriptions being thin when they cover only narrow pieces of territory, leaving out potentially useful information. I believe that without emotional arousal, our conversations with clients can become awfully thin. Using the idea of MOMENTS helps me remember to regularly bring in this arousal. Thinking about Problem discussions as opportunities to bring forth Problem MOMENTS helps me stay focused on the important distinction between reporting and reexperiencing. Perhaps you can tell from the dialogue that my first MOMENT question brought forth some anger (RAGE), and the second MOMENT, separation anxiety (PANIC/GRIEF). Bringing forth these Problem MOMENTS helps the client affectively experience the effects of the Problem. When Problems and their effects are reexperienced in the room, as opposed to being shared as rhetoric or distant descriptions, the client's experience of the Problem can be directly addressed in the context of a therapeutic relationship.

What I am suggesting is that it is important to bring forth the affect first, before linking it to an externalized description. In other words, *affect must be "internalized" before it can effectively be externalized.* By *internalized* I mean that clients must become aware of the affective experience present in their body; if this is not the case, then the externalization might not have the desired effect of helping the clients notice the Problem in a way that strongly invites them to take a position against it. Once affect is internalized, using externalization to link prefrontal cortex "words" with limbic firing accomplishes what Siegel (2011) suggested has the effect of soothing the firing, the aforementioned "name it to tame it." If there is no firing, there is no soothing. MOMENTS, or other practices designed to bring the awareness of feelings into the body, sets this process in motion and creates what David Epston (2014) called a "felt understanding."

If you don't see and feel emotional output, then your clients likely aren't experiencing the effects of the Problem in a way that would have them attend to it differently. Externalization then becomes merely an act of rhetoric and a less meaningful process. Some common situations that should have you on special alert to attend to this distinction are as follows:

Clients who come in with rigid left-hemisphere control*, in other words, under the influence of Perfection or Obsessive-Compulsive Problems.
Those who don't regularly experience feelings in their bodies.
Clients who are somewhat to significantly dissociated (although it will take some work to have them access MOMENTS).
Although it might be counterintuitive, clients who are regularly excitable and/or rage-filled may be easily captured by emotion but might need some help in anchoring these feeling in their bodies in a manageable way before tying them to words.

From an IPNB perspective, these are all situations when the mind is protecting the brain from toxic overload by dis-integrating the link from the right hemisphere to the left, the link from the body to the brain, or the links that allow conscious processing of experience. With these Problems, extra work is required to bring forth, into our client's bodies, the affect we are trying to link to externalized descriptions.

The following is an interesting example of what I think of as a therapist creating an in-session MOMENT:

   T: Well, how does it have you feeling? Does it make you sad?
 ˙ C: Not sure.

Later:

   C: It does make me sad.
   T: Where is it in your body? Is it here, or there, or there? Where is it?
   C: (chooses the heart out of a range of choices) Here.
   T: What's it like when you're feeling that sadness in your heart?
   C: I feel alone at this time.

Now, the client has never given voice to these understandings about life; this is entirely new. So, once again, this is an achievement: the client is linking these acts of violence to "hurting," to sadness, to where that touches the client's body, to being all alone in life—and these are all new developments.

You might find it surprising that the therapist here was Michael White (2011, p. 120). He seemed to think that his work with a young client perpetrating violence could not move forward without the client experiencing the effects of the Problem on himself, before he could experience the effects of what he was doing on others. It appears that White was following the affect (which he was quite masterful at) or, in this case, the lack thereof.

To give another example, my client Dr. G, a really sensitive and caring former boy genius math professor, could articulate the distress he was in but could not actually feel it in his body. His use of feeling words was quite misleading at first, but it eventually became clear that the way he talked about Problems, despite using the right words, was actually experience distant. It would be quite easy to proceed along the usual Narrative lines (which I did for a while) without realizing that the externalizations that were being used weren't emotionally connected to him. He was engaged, gave the usual verbal cues that he was resonating with what we were doing, and was very responsive to me personally. When I realized something was not happening, I went to a greater use of pictures, images, and questions that invited him to pay attention to what was going on in his body (these interventions bring in the right brain, discussed in more detail in later chapters). Instead of using Perfection as an externalized description (he was having trouble completing tasks, as his efforts were Never Good Enough), I asked him to come up with an image—Black Clouds brought more feeling into his body. Not surprisingly, this made him uncomfortable at first, but this discomfort was helpful to his experiencing the Problem in a new way.

To restate the point again (repetition is important to memory formation), it is critical to resist the temptation to label the Problem too quickly, before making sure the externalized description is linked affectively. Without this linkage, we will not achieve the effect we are hoping for: the Problem will not be effectively captured and then separated out. Eliciting Problem MOMENTS is a useful strategy for accomplishing this linkage.

Emotion-Focused Therapists also make use of their version of MOMENTS. In their book *Working With Narratives in Emotion-Focused Therapy*, Angus and Greenberg (2011) classified four types of stories. The first of the two that directly bear on my work they label Same Old Stories, which they suggested are repetitive, flat, and low in personal agency. They suggested that when hearing this kind of story, eliciting autobiographical memories (in other words, distant-past Problem MOMENTS) is useful, and presented research linking access to these memories with good treatment outcomes. Their experience was that once these emotions and the stories linked to them are accessed, then other emotional responses and stories can be accessed, facilitating the development of new self stories. A second category, Empty Stories, comprises stories that are full of details about what happened but stripped of emotional content and without much subjective experience (recall Dr. G). Angus and Greenberg suggested responding to these stories with body questions and deepening "evocative empathy" (i.e., thickened attunement). They quoted research suggesting that poor treatment outcomes are associated with the continued presence of a high percentage of these stories. One conclusion that might be drawn from their work and mine is that we need to access moments and use body questions when there is little emotion, and to construct verbal narratives only when these emotions are elicited, or when they are already strongly present but unanchored by narrative structure. Merely having clients tell stories can invite the kinds of descriptions that are not affect filled.

Angus and Greenberg's treatment outcome research suggested the following:

The combination of high emotional arousal and reflection on the aroused emotion predicted good treatment outcomes, better than either one alone.

Therapists' depth of experiential focus influenced client experience and predicted outcome.

If 25 percent of the session involved moderately to highly aroused emotional expression, this produced good results.

They concluded that productive narrative processing of emotion predicts the best outcomes; experiencing emotions and then building narratives around them contribute to the best results.

Bringing forth MOMENTS is a tool I use to make sure that the work I do with clients maintains a steady amount of emotional arousal. It is often helpful to invite the client to begin by describing the context of the MOMENT. When I said to Matt, "Can you take me through the moment the last time that happened?" he replied with enough detail that I could see that he was really picturing what was occurring. If he had just said, "I saw a text from her ex," I might have replied, "Sorry to interrupt, but if it's OK, I would like to slow you down . . . take me through what happened in detail, as if you were picturing it. When exactly did this happen, where were you, can you remember what you were wearing?" There is a quality of reverie when clients are back in the MOMENT—you can feel it happening in the room. If the Problem involves a dampening or disconnection from the client's embodied experience, you might have to work harder to make these MOMENTS happen. In extreme instances, you may have to go really slowly into the MOMENT or approach one a little bit at a time. Clients will usually signal that they have had all they can tolerate by changing the subject or showing frustration with trying to stay in the MOMENT even for a short time. I always make it okay to move on from this conversation, acknowledging their effort, as well as the Problem's power to make accessing these MOMENTS difficult.

Listening in MOMENTS is like listening and responding to any story in Narrative Therapy. This usually involves asking questions in response to people's experience, often guided loosely by the Statement of Position map. It also involves "double-listening": while discussing the Problem we look for agency, both in action and in feelings, in how the client is dealing with the Problem. Although often not visible to the client, eventually these agentive anti-Problem responses will be useful as a contrast to the Problem-influenced conclusions about themselves or others. For example, when Matt said, "I text with her about this to get her to prove her love," I made a mental note to return to this, as I believe it represented a knowledge Matt had (that she did love him) that was subjugated by the Problem. As an aside, if no such anti-Problem responses are apparent in the story, therapists can inquire about or listen for preferences for how the clients want to feel, or what they would like to have done or have someone else do instead; these can also be eventually contrasted with the Problem experience.

Before asking a question in a MOMENT, I often make an attuned response to clients (e.g., "That pain must be really hard to deal with"). This conveys that I am experientially following them, accentuates their emotional response, and brings it directly into the context of our relationship. Bringing forth MOMENTS facilitates attunement as it brings more affect into the conversation. One can also convey attunement through tone of voice, facial expressions, body language, and the content of the next question (as we have traditionally done in Narrative Therapy), but what I am encouraging is to respond directly to the affect. Narrative therapists might react to this type of editorializing comment as both retro (the kind of before Narrative comment we were taught to make) and internalizing as opposed to externalizing (at the end of this chapter I give a rationale for this kind of response). As the conversation about the MOMENT goes on, it is important to continue to make sure the client's experience is affectively grounded; you may have to keep checking in with the client if this isn't apparent, and redirecting toward experiencing the MOMENT and the affect that it brings forth. One way I do this is by slowing the client down, suggesting that I can't keep up—meaning that I've not been able to get a sense of the client's affective experience.

Here are some of the kinds of questions to ask after bringing the client into a Problem MOMENT. These are guided by the Statement of Position map and a focus on affect:

1. When you experience the Problem, what are the effects?
In my conversation with Matt, I felt it was critical that I make sure that he was staying in touch with the affective experience of the effects of the Problem. To do so, I continually invited him to be mindful of his body and regularly solicited Problem MOMENTS that were examples of the effects he was naming. With Matt, the first MOMENT revolved around a way that Insecurities influenced him ("Can you take me through the moment the last time that happened?"). I then made sure he was still in the MOMENT before asking him about what was in his body ("Can you picture the moment when Insecurities got you imagining that? What was going on in your body?"). Matt's response ("I was thinking about the

pain of her breaking up with me") acknowledges the pain the Problem got him to imagine having, to get him to react in ways that support the Problem (e.g., "I told her to call me when she was really broken up"). These Problem-encouraged reactions then have real effects on the relationship (e.g., they didn't speak for several days after), on his girlfriend (e.g., she began to experience herself in the same painful ways she had in her previous relationship), and on Matt (e.g., he experiences Inadequacies and more Insecurities). This is a really good example of how Problems generate negative affect (in this case the Panic of loss) in persons' bodies to solicit their cooperation, and why it is so important to bring these feelings directly into awareness.

2. What past emotional experiences feel similar to those that just came up in the Problem MOMENT?

Linking affective experiences garnered from Problem-influenced MOMENTS over time strongly invites clients to notice what the affective experience is like under the influence of the Problem. A scaffold is formed that helps clients become more aware of something that they already "knew." In addition, bringing forth multiple instances over time usually has the effect of clients realizing that what they are experiencing may not be only from what is happening now.

From the standpoint of neurobiology, our brains tend to "chunk" information (Levitin, 2006) in a way that results in generalized predictions of future events. Experiences with strong affect behind them have more influence in this brain process, especially if they bring a sense of threat. It is no wonder that Problems can have such a strong advantage. The predictions they make to ensure cooperation from the client are backed by neurobiological processes that make these expectations feel as if they are true.

To return to Matt as an example, he had already told me that he tends to "unilaterally end the relationship because I find reasons not to trust them." So I asked him to share a MOMENT with me from one of those relationships that was similar to his current Problem-influenced experience: "Can you tell me about a time when you felt that pain in a previous relationship?" As he was going through the MOMENT, he got in touch with the pain he had experienced, remarking, "I don't want to feel this way anymore." I then wondered if he experienced something similar in any other kinds of relationships he was involved in. He denied having the Problem with friends or at work. I filed this away to return to later, wondering to myself how he was able to keep the Problem out of these relationships. At this time, he did not offer anything about relationships from earlier in his life.

3. What (cultural) factors support power?

This is an especially generic version of this question. Deconstructing Problems, that is, bringing forth the (cultural) factors that are supporting the Problem, has long been a mainstay of Narrative work. This focus reflects the influence of Foucault, as well as the inclination of Narrative Therapists to bring forth the operations of power by understanding and locating Problems in their sociopolitical context (as opposed to in individuals or in families). In effect, cultural specifications about gender, race, class, or sexual preference may be providing a context in which the Problem flourishes. Yet, in my experience, nowhere is the emphasis on bringing forth embodied, affectively-laden experience more needed in Narrative Therapy than in deconstructing Problems. Without eliciting our clients' emotionally embodied experience, they will respond to these types of questions with cultural rhetoric as opposed to experience-near responses.

I gave examples of these types of questions earlier with Matt, so I'll share an experience I had with a woman who was a CEO and who consulted me about her marital difficulties. She said that her husband had instructed her to get the help she needed to improve the marriage. She was concerned about not being able to meet all her husband's needs for attention and home management and was worried that she was not capable of being a good wife. When I began to ask her about her experience and understanding of how women were encouraged to be and feel in this culture, she told me that she understands that women are unfairly culturally encouraged to feel selfish if they do not focus on loved ones' needs at the expense of their own, but in her particular case she actually *was* selfish for not giving more. While she clearly got the concept of women's lack of entitlement intellectually, her personal emotional response was still influenced by this dominant social discourse. To address her emotional response, I asked her to find a MOMENT when she felt selfish. When in the MOMENT, she was able to feel the pain of having her own needs put aside. Here are some of my questions:

"As you are picturing him making these demands on you, what's hap-
    pening in your body?"
"How are you experiencing him at this time?"
"What's it like to have your own dreams be put aside?"

Once she was in a Problem MOMENT, I was able to effectively ask questions that helped locate the entitlement and power operations of her partner. I asked her about other experiences in her life when acting with entitle-ment evoked negative affect, either personal MOMENTS or MOMENTS when she witnessed other women (like her mom) learning that lesson: "Tell me about a time when you've seen other men responding to you or other women in this way"? When sharing these Problem MOMENTS with me, the pain of her experience thickened, and she no longer viewed these situations from either the Problem's or her husband's point of view.

In general, when we ask these questions in moments, clients are more in touch with their own and others' emotional experience and less likely to give an intellectual justification for their own behavior or for their participation in dominant culturally encouraged behavior.

4. What ways are you experiencing the Problem now?

This is a variant of the standard evaluation question used to invite the client to take a position against the Problem, but asked in a more experience-near, in-the-moment way. Asking these questions while cli-ents are wrapped up in a MOMENT allows them to access their experi-ence of the Problem and not just their conclusions about it; their felt experience of the Problem tends to generate a response that is more embodied and better able to compete with the emotion-based way the Problem is influencing them.

Matt: I don't like the way Insecurities are making me act and how
         this is making my girlfriend feel . . . It's mean.

Clearly the direction the Problem had taken Matt had led him to respond in ways that stood against his own values; noticing this supported his stance that the Problem was "mean."

5. What personal values or hopes and dreams of yours are affected by the Problem?

This type of question thickens the stance against the Problem by inviting a justification of the client's new position. Once again, when a client is asked this type of question while experiencing a Problem MOMENT, what gets thickened is the affect involved in the client's stance.

Once I got Matt in touch with his feelings about how he was acting, and the effects his actions had on his girlfriend, it was easy to get him to reflect on how his behavior stood against his preferred way of being:

J: Why do you feel that Insecurities are mean?
M: Well I really don't want to treat women that way . . . or anybody that way.

When I asked him to share a MOMENT when he had witnessed someone important to him treating him or others in a way he valued, he told me a story about his aunt giving him attention and understanding in a situation where he was being difficult. Being in the MOMENT had him reliving the experience, and there were tears in his eyes as he shared the experience with me. As suggested, these re-membering questions add a "member" to the preferred story. Re-membering questions are often emotionally evocative no matter how you ask them because they elicit memories of specific relational experiences. Memories that have a lot of emotions behind them tend to have more influence.

6. Can you picture a MOMENT, an experience in the future, that could occur if your relationship with the Problem remains unchanged? Describe this to me as you are imagining it.

I never needed to ask Matt this question because of how the work evolved, but if I was having difficulty getting him to notice the Problem's hurtful influence, I might have asked:

"Let's say six months or a year from now I run into you and the Problem is still around. Can you describe for me a scene from your relationship where Insecurities is still getting you to treat your girlfriend in ways you don't actually approve of?"

This type of question creates an experience of what might be in store for the client if things continue to go as they have been going, and can be a useful question for assisting the client in further separating from the Problem.

7. What's happening in your body right now? Can you tell me where you feel the Problem in your body?

I have found this question to be useful anytime, inside or outside of a MOMENT. When I asked Matt, "Can picture the moment when Insecurities got you imagining that? What was going on in your body," he gave me more of a general response: "I was thinking about the pain of her breaking up with me." I chose not to pursue this further, as there was a pained look in his face when he responded.

But I could have followed up with, "Can you show me exactly where this pain is in your body?" This type of question invites mindful awareness to the body, which facilitates the client noticing bodily based responses when the Problem is around. This increased awareness allows clients, over time, to notice when the Problem shows up in the body and to respond to it, facilitating greater management of the Problem. It also allows clients to notice their overall experience more readily, which reduces the Problem's influence on their life. We will look more closely at the use of body awareness and mindfulness in Chapter 4. Chapters 5 and 6 look at the usefulness of raising these bodily based questions in the context of what is happening in the client-therapist relationship.

8. As you are noticing what's happening in your body as the Problem takes over you, do you feel a surge of energy, or perhaps feel your energy being drained away?

In addition to locating the Problem in the body, noticing either the surge of energy or the depletion of energy that occurs along with the presence of the Problem can also be useful in managing the Problem. Once clients notice this arousal in the body and share it with the therapist, they can learn to manage and regulate it, which will help them eventually to respond in a more preferred manner. I discuss this and how it relates to the body's response to stress in Chapter 6.

Although many of these are standard Narrative Therapy questions, asking them in a MOMENT maintains the client's lived experience as the backdrop of the discussion. Of course, the timing of questions is critical, but if you are following the client rather than the map of questions, you'll find the right type of question to ask. Michael White used to tell a story in workshops about a therapist who rang him up (this was back in the day, before much e-mail) and told him that he'd gone down the list of questions (from White, 1988), asking his client each one, with predictably poor results.

Unique Outcome MOMENTS

Most traditional therapy models attempt to capture and manage negative affect, while newer models are about supporting and developing positive affect. Narrative Therapy has practices that do both. When responding to new developments in clients' lives, I now look to enter into not Unique Outcomes but Unique Outcome MOMENTS (UOMs), as this helps me to remember to invite the client into a richly storied description of what was going on. Going through a UOM creates a context in which clients reexperience the positive affects associated with their efforts. I am trying to move Reauthoring conversations filled with experience-distant descriptions, explanations, and conclusions to conversations that involve affectively rich experiences in the room. Otherwise, we can end up getting details of the story that do not contain much affect, and we might miss the opportunity to have clients reexperience their delight in the context of a caring relationship and witness.

Like working with Problem MOMENTS (and perhaps more important), entering into UOMs means inviting a rich description of the entire set of circumstances, with as much detail as possible to recreate the context of the event. Using Narrative language, when Problems are big and have been around a while (and thus highly influential), it can take some work to bring forth UOMs, as the Problem's influence will make it difficult for UOMs to be brought forth and experienced with the therapist.

How might we understand this difficulty from an IPNB point of view? New developments in the client's story occur in similar situations in which the Problem is performed. As some of the same cues are involved with both the Problem and these new developments, the brain will not easily discriminate between them. In addition, to the extent that the person experiences the influence of the Problem at the same time as taking steps away from the Problem, then with these steps can come both the positive affect of victory and the Problem-influenced experience of danger. Entering into the UOM means entering into an alternative brain state*, different from the one that supports the Problem. With more experience behind it, and because negative affect takes precedence over positive affect, when inviting a client to step into a UOM the Problem brain state may be more easily triggered, bringing with it negative affect and pulling the conversation in another direction. As memory retrieval is influenced by our current emotional state, we are more likely to remember those times that feel similar to how we are currently feeling. If the feeling behind the Problem is evoked, or if the client is in the grip of the Problem during the conversation, it will be difficult to access memories of good-feeling events.

Persistence on the therapist's part is also necessary for working with those who have the hardest time accessing and staying inside MOMENTS. The Problem that influences these clients is often one that involves disconnection from their feelings. Bringing forth MOMENTS means bringing forth feelings that they are not used to feeling. Davidson and Begley (2012) suggested that self-awareness is mediated by the insula, which connects signals from all over the body to the brain. Experience shapes these connections. When you have experiences in life where you learned that it was safer not to feel, then it feels too dangerous to easily experience any strong affect, including positive affect. In general, slowing things down, breathing, and carefully going through the specific details of the UOM will help prevent the Problem from interfering with the UOM. With some clients, your initial work with MOMENTS might usefully focus on in-session MOMENTS only, as they bring the client into the here-and-now and so into the room with a caring, supportive therapist.

Additionally, for clients who enter therapy with clear descriptions of ways they have already begun to leave the Problem behind, the therapeutic conversation is more about thickening this new direction by soliciting UOMs. For other clients who, in the beginning of the work, cannot tolerate the negative feelings associated with talking about the Problem, starting instead with their preferences for life, or their hopes and dreams, may be a safer alternative. Only once a foundation of these possibilities is built for them to stand on (i.e., lots of good affect has been evoked) and safety is constructed in the relationship, is it then possible to talk about the Problem and manage the associated negative affect that this brings. Diana Fosha's (2013) work on building from positive emotions would likely be of great interest for Narrative Therapists. She suggested a moment-to-moment processing of experiences of positive change, done with the same rigor devoted to processing Problems. Like Narrative Therapists, she likes to focus on what the client experiences as therapeutic. For her, experiences to process include those in the client's life, as well as experiences in the session, and the experience of the experience of exploring these moments in the therapist-client relationship.

Here are examples from my work with Matt of following both a UOM and an in-session moment in our relationship. Later in the same session:

J: You said that you get her to prove her love. How does she do that?
M: I know she loves me.
J: Can you tell me about a moment when this was obvious to you?
M: Yesterday . . .
J: OK, let's take this slowly . . . first tell me where you were.
M: In my backyard.
J: Could you paint me a picture of the scene, what you were wearing, what your girlfriend was wearing?

Matt describes the back of his house, the garden, and what they were wearing. Then we continue:

J: Can you sit back and picture this for yourself? I'm interested in what happened in the room, frame by frame, like a movie . . . like you were experiencing it for the first time.

M: Well, we came out to sit on the bench . . .

J: Are you picturing this?

M: OK (closes his eyes) . . . Yes, I can see it . . .

J: Are you two sitting close to each other? Can you smell her perfume?

M: Yes . . . we are talking as we walk out of the house . . . I'm happy to be with her . . . (clearly remembering, now smiling) We are sitting together on the bench under the gazebo . . . I love being next to her . . . (with my encouragement giving me more details of their time together) . . . the last couple weeks have been good . . .

J: (smiling) Good how?

M: (with a warm tone) We were close . . . (still caught up in the moment).

J: (after a bit) What's it like for you to share that closeness with me now?

M: (almost smiling) Not something I do a lot . . . but (nodding) it's OK.

When I got to the point in the session where this piece of the dialogue picks up, I thought that it might be possible to go to a UOM. I felt a small shift; Matt had started to use externalizing language and seemed to be regarding the operations of Insecurities with increased suspicion. In most of my sessions I like to notice a place that might open a door to an alternative story, so I can refer to the possibility of it in my end-of-session summary. I believe that being able to refer to "two stories," one Problem influenced and one in line with a person's preferences, creates a useful juxtaposition of Old and New Stories and invites the client to have hope. For example, this UOM brought forth feelings of care and connection for Matt and provided a useful template for a counterstory (Closeness) that we could use throughout the therapy. For Matt, closeness means feeling connected, safe, and secure.

Narrative Therapists might find the specific focus on my relationship with my client ("What's it like for you to share that closeness with me now?") to be incongruent with the Narrative practice of holding a decentered stance. One way to look at this from a Narrative Therapy perspective is that I am becoming part of his membered team, one that supports closeness in his personal relationships, including the one between him and me. From an IPNB perspective, I was providing an alternative experience of attachment* for him. Theoretical viewpoints aside, my experience in the room was one of greater connection between me and Matt after the above interchange. I was hoping that this development would contribute to greater safety for him in our relationship (remember the Problem is Insecurities). This became an in-session UOM, a lived experience that was different from what the Problem would encourage.

Here are some different kinds of questions to ask after bringing the client into a UOM. As with Problem MOMENTS, these are guided by the Statement of Position map and a focus on affect. These are mostly in generic format.

1. Were there other times, perhaps in the past, when you felt similar to how you are feeling now?

Responses to this type of question provide an emotionally based scaffold that can support a new direction. After eliciting a MOMENT, I often like to track the history of several similar MOMENTS before going to the more standard Narrative Reauthoring questions. Bringing forth similar-feeling UOMs from different points in time puts the affective experience on firmer ground. For example, Matt's was able to recall a number of experiences with his girlfriend when he felt close.

Given that negative affect can have such a strong influence, I believe we have to work extra hard to build a foundation of good affect to compete with the Problem story. Narrative Therapists' use of letter writing and Outsider Witness groups contribute to the same end. I suspect that this is why White and Epston found that these interventions had such useful effects. They increased positive affect, which helped counter the Problem story (their informal research found a letter to be worth four sessions and an Outsider Witness group experience to be worth ten sessions). White and Epston placed great importance on these practices to accomplish the goals of their work.

2. As you are picturing these times of responding in preferred ways, can you think of a name for this new direction or an image that represents it? . . . Let's take a breath together and consider what you

have just named. Does this name/image bring up other images, other times?

Matt was able to picture the scene with his girlfriend on the bench as representative of a New Story of "Closeness." Each time we met, we found several of these to add to the New Story. With some clients, I have actually asked them to take pictures with their cell phones that captured these kinds of MOMENTS. Images are more likely than words to bring forth affect, as they are mediated by the right hemisphere.

The specific questions in the next categories use content from Matt's story. Of course, you would substitute your client's story content while keeping the basic question format.

3. Re-membering questions: Who would be the least surprised to know that you have this preference for Closeness (in Matt's case), for treating people in warm, caring ways? Let's pick a MOMENT from your time with that person.

Matt returned to some positive experiences with his aunt. We went over a couple of significant MOMENTS between the two of them, and brought forth both the meaning these experiences contributed to Closeness, and the practices they engaged in that support connection.

4. Traditional Narrative questions about effects, evaluation, and justification: What are the effects of Closeness (in Matt's case)? What do these effects leave you thinking or feeling about Insecurity versus Closeness? How does Closeness represent a better fit for you in your life?

Each of these different types of questions is asked in a manner that privileges lived experience by asking for MOMENTS that reflect the client's experience.

5. Questions that bifurcate both the Problem and the alternative developments.

How did Closeness get you to change your reaction in that situation, and how is this different from how insecurities have gotten you to react in similar situations (in Matt's case)?

I find these types of questions very useful in sharpening the distinction between the Problem and the alternative story, and particularly useful when contrasting Problem and New Story MOMENTS. With Matt, I often went from MOMENTS of Closeness and Caring back to MOMENTS when Insecurities got him to react in hurtful ways. You will see examples of bifurcated questions with other clients later in the book. As discussed in Zimmerman and Beaudoin (2015), the neurobiology of bifurcation involves pairing a stronger neural firing (an example of the Problem) with a neural firing that you want to make stronger (an anti-Problem development) to thicken the alternative firing. Bifurcation questions are popular in many models (for a discussion of them in Milan Therapy, see Tomm, 1984).

6. Future-looking-back questions: If you come back next week, and Insecurities are gone again, what experiences will you share with me that reflect this change? . . . If I run into you in, say, six months or a year from now?

These types of question are useful in situations when the Problem went away but then returned. It invites clients to remind themselves what might be possible if they move back in an anti-Problem direction. Asking these questions with MOMENTS involves not only bringing forth and reviewing the skills and knowledge involved in leaving the Problem behind but also bringing back anti-Problem experiences. For example, if Matt comes back to talk with me, complaining that Insecurities have made a comeback, we would enter into MOMENTS (both past and current) that represent either a departure from Insecurities or an embracement of Closeness, and reflect the attitudes and practices involved in either.

7. What's happening in your body right now?

Once again, I have found this question to be useful anytime in any kind of MOMENT. Noticing sensations in the body that occur during discussions of new developments can encourage the client and reinforce the therapeutic work. When Matt said (with a warm tone), "We were close," I could have reflected, "I got a really warm feeling from you when you said that. Did it feel warm to you? Where is the warm feeling in your body? Have you had warm feelings like that in your body before?"

8. When you began to feel either a surge of energy or the energy going out of your body, how did you manage to hold on to yourself and respond in a preferred manner? What went into this development? . . . What would you call the state your body was in when Closeness was present? How would you compare this to what you've experienced when Insecurities have gotten hold of you?

These questions invite the client to notice the contrast between the experience of physical arousal that supports the Problem and the arousal experience of responding in a preferred manner. Directing attention to this experience invites clients to be more mindful of their bodily based reactions. The first two questions are useful when the client shares a MOMENT when the Problem started to get hold of them but they were able to escape it. It also becomes an opportunity to interview the client about the skills and knowledge they have for effectively managing arousal. The second two questions invite the client to process the positive affect associated with an anti-Problem experience and compare it to the experience of being under the influence of the Problem.

For example, at his next session two weeks later, Matt reported a "decent" couple of weeks. We went through a small Problem MOMENT and then a few situations when he could have "lost it" but didn't. When I asked about these developments, Matt told me that when he started to feel the Insecurities in his body, he was able to remember how he wanted to respond to the person he loved. Because they were minor incidents (stressful, but not overwhelmingly threatening), he was able to hold on to the work we did by using a left-brain cognitive approach to handle the Problem arousal. If the incident had been bigger, the arousal would have been too difficult for him to manage, as we still needed to do more work on what this "bigger" affect felt like to him.

Summary: Affect

Whether discussing Problems or developments, I now believe it is necessary to first generate a strong affective base (through MOMENTS, if needed). I often thicken this experience by connecting it to other similar affective experiences and by locating it in the body. Only then do I invite the client to name it in an externalized way. And only after this has been accomplished do I begin to shift the conversation toward exploring the identity conclusions the person has taken from dominant cultural discourse.

Here are some "formulas" you might find useful summaries of these ideas:

Affect-filled Problem memories externalized and named + Story = Problem management

Affect-filled Unique Outcome memories reexperienced + Story = New Story

And here is revised (or, as a colleague of mine suggested, a more "modern") Statement of Position map:

Problem	Developments
Current experience	Alternative experience
Affective experiences—Problem MOMENT	Affective experience—UOM
Past experiences—past and distant past Problem MOMENTS	Past experiences—past and distant past Unique Oucome MOMENTS
Name Problem	Re-membered others—MOMENTS
Effects—MOMENTS	Name New Story
Evaluation/justification/future—MOMENTS	Effects, etc.—MOMENTS

To summarize:

- Not accounting for emotions in therapy leaves you swimming upstream. Emotions are the underlying operating system, orienting our attention, providing energy and motivation. Emotions are what generate stories; when talking without emotion, you are not directly connected to the brain systems that generate Problems.

- MOMENTS, MOMENTS, MOMENTS. Internalizing affect first results in maximum effectiveness and generates access to rich descriptions. In the room, this sounds and feels very different from explanations, conclusions, and reviews of events. When someone tells a story that is affectively rich, I am transported into the experience with them; otherwise, I find myself thinking about what they told me from a more experience distant and cognitive position.

- Collecting MOMENTS is also useful for scaffolding affect when asking questions encouraged by the Statement of Position map (see above). Entering into them at a pace that slowly increases arousal helps the client begin to tolerate stronger and stronger affect. In-session MOMENTS aid in the project of scaffolding affective tolerance as well.

- Bifurcation rules! We know that neurons that fire together wire together. However, to maximally invite the wiring to occur, the Problem/New Story bifurcation must be done with strong affect. For example, in the couple of sessions that followed our initial one, Matt and I reviewed a MOMENT when Insecurities got the better of him, and then a MOMENT when he was able to take a stand and not let Insecurities get him to respond in ways that had negative effects, and then another Insecurities-influenced MOMENT, and another when he took a stand, and so on.

- Deconstruct lived experience, not conclusions. Inviting conclusions (e.g., I know that woman are "supposed" to be selfless) won't evoke the experiences people have had that influence their cooperation with the dictates of dominant cultural discourse. Perhaps the process through which these discourses become internalized occurs when a person experiences directly or sees modeled punishing responses to breaking these dictates. This learning comes with Fear, which is then stored in memory. As the negative affect is strong, so is the influence of these memories. This negative affect provides the energy behind self-surveillance and encourages future performances of dominantly prescribed versions of the self. The affect must be accessed first to begin to have the deconstructing effects we want.

- Building from the positive requires maximum effort! Given that negative affect tends to rule the day, you must go to all possible lengths (e.g., Outsider Witness groups, letters, certificates, lots of remembering questions) to build support for alternative stories and positive affect. Letter-writing campaigns (Madigan, 2011) provide relational support to positive affect through participants sharing evocative good memories with the client. Collective narrative practices involve working with entire communities to achieve a similar effect.

Curious about what happened with Matt? We had two more sessions over the next month, and then another one month later. On that visit he reported, in an affectless tone, that it had been a "rough month" with "big" anxiety moments. I asked him to take me through a Problem moment, and he entered into a clearly evocative one that revolved around an experience in San Diego. He and his girlfriend had entered a bar, and when he stopped to go to the bathroom, and his girlfriend said, "I'll just go on and meet you at the bar."

J: So you are beginning to open the bathroom door, and Claire was turning the corner . . .

M: Yeah, I just began to lose it . . . my head was pounding . . . I began yelling at her.

J: It was too hard for you; you lost control.

M: I was imagining her going to the bar and finding some other guy to pay attention to.

J: That must have been horrible for you . . . Did this situation feel familiar to you in any way?

M: When I was younger, I always tried to play it safe; I was a middle child (crying now); my parents couldn't care less.

When Matt was in San Diego and this incident occurred, I imagine it put him over the edge of his window of tolerance*; he simply lost higher cortical control and became emotionally reactive to the situation. When he shared it with me as a Problem MOMENT, he entered an emotional space I hadn't seen him in before: his face turned red, and there was a weight of emotion in his voice. For the first time he even described to me what was happening inside of him without me asking.

When I said, "It was too hard for you; you lost control," my intention was to strongly internalize Matt's affect before beginning to externalize it. Instead of the common Narrative Therapy practice of editorializing about the Problem (e.g., "Insecurities really got a hold of you") followed by a question, I engaged in what I think of as an emotional editorialization. I believe that this type of response is useful with clients whose emotions need to be thickened. This is more than empathy—it is an invitation to fully enter into emotions that are already flowing around

their bodies, but not necessarily storied. The goal here is to first bring
forth these emotions so they can be accessed, named, externalized, and
storied.

Notice that when I said, "That must have been horrible for you,"
instead of asking him, "What was that like for you?" I named his experience for him, rather than asking him to make meaning of it. This raises
an interesting question of the possibly different effects between those
two possible therapeutic responses. Is one more evocative? Is one more
supportive? How does each affect my relationship with my clients and
their relationship with themselves? Do I center the relationship to facilitate a shared emotional experience, or do I remain warmly decentered?
In this situation I took the position of an attuned responder, perhaps
inviting an attachment experience for him with me. I do believe that
the type of response I made better captured Matt's attention, as it mobi-
lized his emotions (remember emotions are a call to the brain to pay
attention), making it more likely to open things up and facilitate a process of changing emotional meanings. Angus and Greenberg claim that,
"Stories emerge from the body when there is a facilitative listener present to receive them" (2011, p.142), but the dilemma of centering or not
remains an interesting question for me. With other clients, it might be
more important to keep privileging their experience with as little colo-
nization by the therapist's response as possible. In the end, I believe that
each kind of response has its time and place and that the freedom to be
flexible is useful. In Matt's case, I believe that choosing to deepen his
emotional response and increase his connection to me allowed him to
access and share the emotional meaning the situation evoked for him:
"When I was younger, I always tried to play it safe; I was a middle child
(crying now); my parents couldn't care less." His making this connection
proved to be a turning point in the work we were doing.

When Matt returned for another session three weeks later, he said
happily that he and his girlfriend had just had "their best three weeks."
When I asked him what went into this, he said that his previous session
"was huge for him," that he had a different appreciation of Insecurities
and how they "used" the lack of attention he had experienced earlier in
his life to "mess with things." He said that he needed to take responsibility and deal with what his Problems were and that whatever Claire did

meant nothing personal about him or her feelings to him. I then invited a UOM of Closeness, during which he concluded, with tons of feeling, "Somebody really loves me."

Narrative Therapists may worry about the effects of situating Problems in a way that negatively implicates parents—we were all concerned about the effects of mother blaming back in the day. However, when I saw him for another session several weeks later, he started out by telling me he rang up his parents for the first time in a while.

I believe that letting his feelings enter his body and conscious mind triggered a process where he began to create new meaning about his past experiences. This new meaning occurred in the present, which allowed it to be more influenced by his present-day memories and experiences and not predominantly by meaning and experience from when he was a child (I discuss this process in Chapter 6). I'd like to also point out that I made no interpretations but, rather, attended to emotionally salient events in a way that invited new meaning. The critical piece of this, though, was that he had to directly experience the stored affect in order to allow to make new reflections on it and not just a cognitive connection.

In Matt's next and final session, we brought forth some specific parent-related moments from the past—this time they were positive memories. This facilitated more restorying of his relationship with them. Through reexperiencing and making new meaning of old events, as well as incorporating new developments, Insecurities began to shift for Matt, allowing Closeness to feel safer to him.

I hope the work with Matt and the theoretical knowledge I described illustrate the importance and usefulness of privileging affect in the therapeutic conversation. Now we turn to the body and the mind.

Chapter **4**

Body/Mindfulness Practices in Narrative Therapy

*Remember, a Jedi's strength flows from the
Force. . . . Life creates it, makes it grow. Its energy
surrounds us and binds us. Luminous beings are
we, not this crude matter. You must feel the Force
around you; here, between you, me, the tree, the
rock, everywhere, yes.*
—Yoda in *The Empire Strikes Back*

Mindfulness, breathing, and embodying are the simple but critical messages in this chapter, illustrated through the story of Doug, a forty-five-year-old Asian American, heterosexual, divorced investment banker, who was having trouble getting work done and was having difficulty with closeness in all of his relationships. I had been working with Doug in traditional Narrative ways and noticed that it wasn't having the effect of separating him from the Problem, or helping him to notice possibilities for Problem management. While Doug was describing intense Anxiety symptoms, he was doing so in a rote manner.

I decided that taking a body/mindfulness approach would help bring forth more affect for Doug, as his life experiences had resulted in his mind blocking access to his internal awareness of his emotions and bodily sensations. The body is where our emotions are first experienced. In general, I find it extremely useful to bring forth the Problem from the body and then ask about its influence. For example, in Chapter 3, after I asked Matt to locate the Problem in his body, he was able to connect his pain with imagining his girlfriend leaving him. When Michael White's client found sadness in his body, he related it to the experience of being alone. For Doug, it would take mindful work to help him experience the emotions in his body.

I also wanted to try to bypass the way his mind used words to obscure his emotional experience. Doug, when reviewing the Problem, offered meaningless causal attributions, relating it to various negative aspects of himself (he had had a lot of therapy in his life). In the first piece of the dialogue below, I use imagery to bring in his right brain more directly. In later dialogues, I use breathing to help him turn off the word chatter and to open him up to more fully experience his difficulties. This idea emerged from my interest and experience in mindful meditation, which quiets the mind and creates space for more bottom-up processing, a "purer" taking in of what our senses are processing, less filtered through previous experience. With top-down processing, in contrast, your mind provides a filtered interpretation of what is occurring.

The following dialogue picks up early in our fourth session, after Doug had once again lapsed into experience-distant rhetoric about his Problem:

> D: Overwhelm . . . Panic . . . I take on too much. I can't get any work done and things are due. I'm avoiding the bigger things—why is that? Why can't I just do it?
>
> J: (Here's where I decided to do something different) Close your eyes and try to picture this Avoidance. What does it look like? What comes up when you do this?
>
> D: Failure, risking failure . . . dread.
>
> J: Failure?
>
> D: I'll be revealed, exposed. I'll let them down.
>
> J: Try picturing this, letting them down.
>
> D: An arena, like with gladiators.
>
> J: You're the gladiator?

D: No, the slave.

J: So you're the slave . . . but what does the bad feeling that comes from letting them down look like, the thing that's going after the slave?

D: Like a hammer . . .

J: Imagine that hammer swinging at you . . . What's in your body?

D: A wave of shittiness . . .

J: Hold on to the wave . . . can you hold it?

D: I think that . . .

J: No, imagine holding the wave, don't think about it.

D: OK, I'm picturing it.

J: Now imagine a helper to handle the wave. What comes up?

D: A shield, a steel shield . . . an umbrella shield.

J: OK, this week, when there is Avoidance getting in your way—failure, feelings, the letting others down thing—imagine the wave, and then the shield . . .

Traditional Narrative Therapy with kids has used imagery and imagination with great success. For example, with children I often have them draw a picture of the Problem, then a picture of what the Problem is doing to them, and then at some point a picture of what they are doing to the Problem. Yet with adults we tend to focus more on words. When the words are presented with little affect, and you have little movement working in "words-land," it's time to do something different. My work with Doug offers body- and mind-oriented possibilities for doing so.

Like most clients when they are asked to put an image to a Problem (or draw a picture of it), Doug depicted himself (the slave) rather than picturing the Problem itself. Once I made the critical distinction for him between him being the Problem and the Problem being the Problem, the Problem became pictured (the hammer) and externalized. I then had him imagine the hammer swinging at him and asked about his body, assuming that the image will bring more feeling into it. He then experienced "a wave of shittiness," which was shared with me with much more affect than before. When I asked him to hold on to the wave, I had to interfere with his immediate inclination to "think" and instead directed him back to the image. Holding on to the wave brought up more affect for him then he could handle without support.

At the end of this sequence I asked him to imagine a helper. I wanted to leave him with something to do to manage the Problem, although it is generally more helpful when solutions and new meanings occur spontaneously (as you saw happen with Matt). Imagery-based work facilitates affective arousal; when feelings come into the body, new possibilities often spontaneously emerge. It would have been probably best to have left him grappling with as much of the wave as he could manage. I could have even suggested that when Avoidance got a hold of him, he might try breathing and picturing the wave (but off in the distance).

In an interesting side note, neuroanalytic therapists attend to the images and metaphors a client might bring in and wonder about their meaning. (In the early days of psychoanalysis there was more of a tendency to interpret them.) This wondering might occur out loud or in their own private reflections, as they watch how these metaphors and images change over the course of therapy (Wilkinson, 2010). What I am doing instead is inviting out images "under the guidance of text." Michael White and David Epston (1990) suggested that the particular question that is asked invites the client to make meaning in particular ways. Images can be used in much the same manner.

Here's what happened in the next session:

D: Still lots of panic and anxiety . . . it's in my body.

J: So sorry to hear that you are still suffering. Tell me what it has been like for you. What effects has the anxiety had?

D: It gets me to escalate inappropriately with others. It puts lots of chatter in my head.

J: The hammer . . .

D: Not really a hammer, more like fog . . . a wave of fog. It saps my energy . . .

J: Where is it in your body?

D: (closing his eyes) In my chest, my stomach, my mouth . . . Why can't I feel affection toward others—my girlfriend, my kids?

J: Picture the wave coming over you.

D: I can't . . . isn't it wrong not to feel . . . what's wrong with me?

Doug was starting to feel the anxiety as a backdrop, like an ever-present fog, but wasn't letting it come in full force. At that point in the work, it was likely too dangerous for him to feel those strong negative emotions directly. Without the affective information, his left brain put things together in a way that concluded that something was wrong with him.

Minds

In Narrative Therapy we talk about giving meaning to experience. It is the mind that provides this meaning; what is this "mind" we have been speaking about?

When in the room with clients, we are working with their minds, with our minds. Dan Siegel (2007, 2010a, 2010b, 2012a, 2012b) has suggested a definition of mind as: " an embodied and relational process that regulates the flow of energy and information" (e.g., Siegel, 2012a, p. 2). Mind emerges from the flow of energy and information and then influences the flow. It emanates from the body and is embedded in relationships. Interpersonal Neurobiology (IPNB) takes a strong relational stance, seeing relationships as the means through which the way we see the world evolves. Lev Vygotsky (1986) suggested a similar idea, that the mind takes in social experience and forms itself. In his writings, Siegel goes on to suggest that the mind uses the brain and relationships to shape itself. This triangle metaphor implies that mind, brain, and relationships are all sides of the same thing, that the mind, "powered" by the brain, is created by experience and generated relationally. As the mind evolves, it shapes and regulates all of our subsequent experience, both individual and relational. Interestingly, in his book *Mind: A Journey to the Heart of Being Human* (2017), Siegel noted the two views of mind, as a social function (citing Vygotsky, Gregory Bateson, and Jerome Bruner) and as a neural function, and offered a view of it as both.

In our brain, energy flows through our neurons and triggers chemical reactions in our synapses. However, this energy flow transcends the body, as it flows between all things, including between each of us. While information is a particular type of energy, Siegel included it in his description of mind as a nod to the importance of language in constructing how our minds evolve and work; information relates to the use of symbols that have meaning beyond the symbol itself (e.g., language). From a Narrative Therapy perspective, Poststructuralism also stresses the importance of language (and texts) to the construction of reality and identity. Siegel (2010a) suggested that the specific flow of energy and information creates shifts in probability patterns, which then make some responses, reactions, thoughts, and feelings more or less likely to occur. This idea bears some similarity to Bateson's idea of restraints, which White employed in his early writings (1986, 1988/89). The way our minds operate arises from this pattern of flow and then regulates or shapes future flow. You might say that this flow constitutes our mental life. What we experience is where this flow takes us.

What else might be important to know to help us appreciate how all of our minds operate? Our brains, for survival purposes, have been organized to become efficient filters, to anticipate and predict. To begin with, bottom-up sensory information enters the brain with a minimum of pre-constructed categorization. The senses—the body—take in these sensory signals. For example, with music, the brain takes in sound waves. A correlated neural firing occurs in response to these signals, which then gets translated by the brain. Unlike with other sensory information, such as color, sounds have specific receptors in the brain for each pitch, because recognizing and decoding different sounds have adaptive value. Yet neural translation is also about experience, as we learn to expect certain combinations of sounds and phrases. Daniel Levitin (2006) suggested that musical compositions often relies on our top-down minds to supply familiar sounds or word sequences to us that may be left out of the song at various points. My favorite example is, if I say, Mary had a little . . . , what did you hear? Lamb, I'm sure. Your mind, having learned through experience, provided the rest of the sentence (an example of top-down processing).

So what we perceive, therefore, is a combination of bottom-up sensory information and experientially derived mental models. In a sense, we are talking about the difference between the experiencing self and the narrative self. Prior learning, filled with memories and emotions, shapes our experience from the top down, and this experience then shapes future experiences. Learning from experience helps us operate efficiently because we anticipate what comes next, but like for Doug, it can lead to unhelpful conclusions (e.g., he's a "failure") and Problem influenced expectations (e.g., "I'll be revealed, exposed. I'll let them down"). We all experience some form of top-down chatter, some of it useful and much of it not. As you are reading this book, how much of the "monkey mind" chatter that you are experiencing is helpful in organizing your thinking, and how much of it is distracting you?

One effect of the ways that the brain organizes and categorizes information is to obscure and distance us from direct experience, from the bottom-up flow, that our minds are interpreting and re-presenting to us. Each of us views the world in idiosyncratic ways, specific to our own minds (although, given the influence of dominant discourse we end up with a great deal of similarity in how we view various aspects of life). For example, most of us know something about what Doug means when he uses the words *overwhelm*, *panic*, or *dread*, but not all of us would have categorized what was happening to him in the same way—we each give somewhat different meaning to our own experience. IPNB gives us an understanding of how the brain works and how the mind evolves. Post-structuralism provides us with an understanding of how to deconstruct the dominant cultural texts that the mind is unfolding through.

If we could learn to access direct experience, the ordinary would become extraordinary, and the domestic would become exoticized. (Interestingly, both White and Siegel have suggested versions of this idea). Ideally, we need both to learn from experience *and* to take in the world with openness. Top-down influences are mind-based implicit filters that shape our perceptions, emotional reactions, and behavioral responses, even what we attend to, without any awareness that this is happening. In some cases this top-down flow can be so constricting that it limits awareness not only of bottom-up sensations but also of other people and even of the self. The information from Doug's emotions arrives in the middle prefrontal cortex (mPFC), the area of the brain responsible for regulating affect and integrating it with thinking and social cognition. But because of the way his mind has evolved, the energy flow from the mPFC influences how much affect is triggered ("overwhelm") and leads him to avoid the tasks that trigger this painful experience. Nevertheless, Doug senses on some level that he is out of control, despite not actually feeling these emotions.

Another way to think about all of this comes from Philip Bromberg (quoting Diane Ackerman): "Conscious awareness is not really a response to the world, it's more of an opinion about it" (2011, p. 38). We have opinions, derived from experience, that we think are truths about the world. Louis Cozolino (2016) suggested that in the half second it takes for information to reach consciousness, it has already been subjected to the interpretations previously embedded in our minds. My client Doug's "opinion" about the world is that it will continue to present him with demands that he will not be able to meet, which will then have extremely painful consequences. Narrative Therapists might describe "mind" by saying that we do not operate with a direct knowledge of the world but instead know life through story. What does it mean on a brain level when we talk about changing these stories?

Neuroplasticity is the ability of the brain to change its structure in response to experience., Experience activates neurons, which turn on genes that enable structural changes to strengthen the connections among activated neurons. In other words, as suggested, neurons that fire together, wire together. Experience strengthens synaptic connections, stimulates neuronal growth, and increases sheathing along axonal lengths to enhance conduction speed of electrical impulses. The amount one practices something new is proportional to the amount of myelin wrapping on the relevant circuits. Experience changes the brain, particularly affective experience in the context of a relationship, because this type of experience puts the brain on high alert.

Neurobiologists believe that interpersonal integration results in neural integration, in other words, that attuned relationships with our clients facilitate neuroplasticity and the growth of integrative fibers. I am sure everyone has had the interpersonal experience, in and out of the office, of having the same thought or the same sudden inclination of where the conversation should go next; this likely reflects some level of neural integration with the other person. Furthermore, tracking bodily based sensations, both ours and our clients', facilitates an externalization of what both minds are producing as we have a greater sense of where the other is at and what influences are occurring at that time. Siegel (2010b) referred to seeing one's own and another's mind as *mindsight*.

Yet, how can we attend to our clients, without undue influence of our own minds, so as to increase the likelihood of forming an integrated, decentered relationship with them? Our synaptic connections have formed neural nets that influence us; we are no less likely to fall in the synaptic shadows from the past than are our clients—our top-down filters influence our intake (Zimmerman & Beaudoin, 2015). What kind of experience is useful in helping us loosen the grip of these influences?

Mindfulness Meditation

One particularly useful experience for separating from top-down influences is focused attention, which engages the mPFC and in turn heightens awareness and contributes to neuroplasticity. Insight, empathy, and intuition require activation of the mPFC. As the integration area of the brain, the mPFC collects information from a wide variety of external and internal inputs. Activity in other regions (cortex, limbic, brainstem, body, other brains/bodies) must be linked here to have awareness; without this linking in the mPFC, this information is lost or not necessarily connected in the moment. For example, Siegel (2012b) suggested that, if all the pieces that contribute to the interaction are not integrated in the mPFC, we could interact with others without being aware that we are engaging in certain ways. This lack of awareness is usually the case for Doug, whose attention is on the pressure he feels instead of on what's happening in the present, around him and with others. What we might take from this neurobiological information is that practices that invite focused attention are very helpful in aiding clients to generate new information, as these practices bring the mPFC online.

Developing a personal practice that involves focusing attention (e.g., mindfulness meditation) allows for greater levels of intrapersonal awareness, which contributes to enhanced self-regulation, interpersonal attunement, and overall feelings of kindness toward oneself and others. Siegel (2007, 2010a) used the acronym YODA—You Observe to Decouple Automaticity—as a way to think about the practice of mindfulness meditation. In other words, paying attention fully to the present moment on purpose, often by first focusing on your breath and then by being open to whatever arises, helps us let go of reactive judgments and expectations. In effect, spending time "in" contributes to being able to see more clearly "out."

White, in discussing scaffolding, said that people need distance from the immediacy of their own experience to problem solve; my experience is that mindfulness meditation accomplishes that effect. Separation is created between our experience of ourselves, our top-down influences, and what is going on around us. When this occurs, Problems are not experienced as the totality of one's being. When I started meditating, I learned to bring my attention totally inward and to breathe from that place, concentrating on my breath and experiencing firsthand this effect of seeing what was happening around me externally, dis-identifying myself from these things. I found Siegel's Wheel of Awareness practice (2010a, 2010b) helpful in this regard. In Narrative terms, the wheel is an externalization practice, as no one part of your experience (Problem saturated or otherwise) dominates; you can pay attention to other parts on the wheel and not get stuck.

Of course, meditation is a central feature in Buddhism; Yoda might say, "Ironic it is" that the pinnacle of modern brain science touts an intervention thousands of years old as the be-all and end-all of interventions. Buddhism suggests that emotionally reactive patterns cause suffering, not the experiences themselves. In other words, while the experience may indeed be painful, suffering is an effect of the reaction to the experience. If one directs energy to attention (i.e., mindfulness meditation) instead of engaging in these reactive patterns, the patterns are dismantled and, in effect, externalized. Buddhists refer to dharma, a return to "original mind" and pristine awareness. Dharma is not something from the television show *Lost* but a return to taking in experience without the top-down filters. Interestingly, Zemeira Singer (personal communication, 2016) noted that Michel Foucault and Poststructuralism share a view that Buddhism also holds: the self, reified in dominant psychological ideas, is a construction; it does not exist as a separate thing. While Poststructuralism takes this up through the lens of language, Buddhism takes all sense experience as the territory to be deconstructed. The process of noticing breath, thought, or sensation of any sort allows us to be less linked to our experiences as the truth of our self. Essentially, our experience becomes externalized, and thus we can begin to develop a sense of freedom from the basic reactivity that leads to Problem development.

Richard Davidson and Sharon Begley (2012) described some of their research projects on mindfulness meditation. In general, these studies equate experience meditating with reduced Anxiety, greater attentional abilities, increased moment-to-moment awareness, and greater activation in brain regions thought to mediate empathy. And not just for long-term meditators but for groups that have been trained to do so for two or three months. They described Jon Kabat-Zinn's (2003) mindfulness-based stress reduction approach as one where nonjudgmental, moment-to-moment awareness is practiced. They suggested that mindfulness training shifts neural pathways, with the effect that fewer signals reach the amygdala, leading to less activation of the negative-emotion right prefrontal cortex, and more reliance on the forward-moving, good-feeling left prefrontal cortex. (Chapter 5 discusses these hemispheric differences.)

Countless books and articles have been written about mindfulness meditation and about the positive effect of meditation on people suffering from all kinds of difficulties. Some notable effects are a reduction in relapse of people who struggle with depression (Teasdale et al., 2000); reduction of anxiety, depression, and stress among cancer patients (Speca, Carlson, Goodey, & Angen, 2000); and reduction in drug and alcohol misuse among incarcerated populations (Marlatt, 2006). It would be impossible to summarize all the research on mindful meditation; included here are only some very basic ideas and my personal experiences.

Singer (personal communication, 2016) believes that the rationale for using mindfulness meditation in conjunction with Narrative psychotherapy cannot be overstated. Her experience is that cultivating mindfulness has the effect of taking therapists out of their own heads and away from attention to lists of questions or predetermined agendas, thereby making it easier to notice the times with clients when a different direction might need to be taken, as well as what kind of direction to take. She went on to suggest that mindfulness also facilitates therapist attunement to embodied, rich, affective sharing from the client, allowing us to ask questions that deepen clients' connections to the emotional experiences they are discussing. In a sense, mindfulness meditation serves as the ultimate experience of deconstruction, because while participating in it you are also noticing what is affecting the interaction and how the interaction is enfolding. The extreme alternative to a mindful interaction is one where you are reacting to what the client is saying without any attention to how you are responding or the effects it is having. Singer's experience is also that the more we know about (from our own mindful explorations) the process of exploring our sometimes dangerous-feeling internal territory, the more we are able to help our clients map their inner terrain.

Along these lines, my personal work involves trying to manage Anxiety, a Problem that is triggered in certain situations. In my meditation sessions I bring Anxiety up—book-writing Anxiety looks like a three-headed giant African spitting cobra. Sometimes, memories of other related experiences come up, and I go through these moments while still in my inside place. Paradoxically, as I am slowly able to allow the image of the Problem to get closer to me (over several meditation sessions), Anxiety becomes more manageable. I breathe, picture, and feel the resistance to letting it get closer, and then breathe and picture some more. Also in these sessions, my time inside involves experiencing calm, warm, peaceful, loving feelings. "Inside" is a place I like to find when I am seeing clients; when I get too caught up in the Problem or the interaction I stop, breathe, and go there. I often have my clients close their eyes and breathe for a bit, and then, while still breathing, explore Problems and developments. I find that working this way facilitates more direct experiencing for them and gives us access to images and associations that might not easily arise otherwise. Breathing allows me to get closer to the edge of their now widened inner place, allowing Problem experiences to be more easily tolerated and dismantled.

Let's return to Doug's previous session:

J: Let's try something: breathing together. Would that be OK?
D: What do you mean?
J: I'm going to slow our breathing down. I'll count and do it with you.
D: OK.
J: (Counting and breathing, several repetitions) . . . Now picture the wave.

D: Pain . . .

J: Picture your girlfriend.

D: I'm holding back . . .

J: And your kids.

D: Shame, hurt . . . *failure.*

J: See if you can pull the wave of pain closer.

D: OK, I can touch it.

J: What's the wave like?

D: It hurts.

J: Can you be with it, hold it?

D: Yes, . . . wait a minute, I can let the wave wash right over me. I think we are onto something!

Breathing allowed Doug to feel in his body what he only knew abstractly and couldn't directly experience. From a Narrative perspective, once the affective experience was in his body, externalizing the Problem, in the form of an image, created space between Doug and the Problem and made it safe enough for him to hang in with it and not just be reactively influenced by it. Without capturing the affect, it would have been only a rhetorical exercise. My questions in the context of imagery-based work with breathing provided a structure that helped Doug find his own way to manage the Problem.

From a Neuro-Narrative perspective, once the affect was in Doug's body, it broke down the Problem of Avoidance, which his mind was using to protect his brain from the toxic chemicals that the chronic stress of having all that pain would generate. Avoidance's great promise is a Devil's pact: I won't let you feel the pain, in return for you sacrificing your goals in life. Once the pain was felt ("it hurts") and brought forth in the context of a supportive relationship, Doug was able to better manage the affect, or regulate* it (Chapter 6 comes back to regulation).

Once the affect is more present, through breathing and imagery work, then the therapeutic process involves following and matching the client's affect and then externalizing it. This process will not only open space for clients to notice new possibilities (as it did Doug) but also begin to influence clients' awareness—they becomes more mindfully aware of both their own and their therapist's mind. A greater joint awareness of content develops, and a deeply resonant interpersonal experience evolves that, as discussed further in Chapter 6, contributes to changing neural structure and to shifting patterns of safety seeking and security. If it feels like this joint experience is not happening—if you don't feel a flow between you and your client—then it is likely that safety has not been constructed in the relationship. You might find the familiar metaphor of scaffolding useful in these kinds of situations, moving more slowly from the client's experience to one that is more co-constructed in the relationship.

What About Us? Some Questions:

As therapists, how might our top-down influences—our minds—affect our ability to resonate with our clients? When we are trying to understand our clients' experiences, there is always the risk of coming to conclusions about them more based on our own experience than on theirs. How do we separate from our own top-down influences enough to let theirs come in with less filtering? My belief is that mindfulness meditation practices not only help open up our clients but also allow us to be more truly open to them. Does an ethic of accountability to our interactions require some greater attention to ourselves?

White (2011) suggested that, although therapy was invariably represented as a one-way process, in fact there was actually no detached, autonomous position and that all parties are constitutive of the therapeutic conversation. IPNB supports this idea, as minds evolve and transact in a relational context. If we truly "take in" our clients' experiences, if we listen with a clear and focused mind, will our responses more likely contribute to an energy flow that will help our clients' minds evolve in ways that will more fit with their preferences? How might that change our minds? If questions aren't the most critical factor in changing Narratives, what is? (I address these questions in Chapter 5.) Perhaps, like professional athletes who need to work out with their bodies for their job, it might be useful for us to do mind workouts.

Here is a question that crystallizes for me what I am talking about: is being decentered a practice, or is it a state of mind*, a coherent, integrated place that we are coming from? If it's a practice, we can listen, follow, be curious, co-create. But if it's a state a mind, perhaps the difference is that we *feel* decentered! We feel the energy flow between us and our clients, and in our bodies. What I try to remember is that co-creation is not just a word—it is embodied and felt.

For me, meditation experiences have not only contributed to my ability to separate from my top-down influences but also increased my ability to connect to my body. The insula, where the body is represented in the brain, is the seat of energy management, of emotional regulation, of mirror neurons*, and of moment-to-moment tracking of fluctuations of the *felt* sense of affective experiences. Doing a body scan is a common meditation practice; I think of it as weight lifting for the insula. This practice has increased the strength of my connection to my own bodily based responses. What makes bringing our own bodies and our clients' bodies into our Narrative work so useful and important? Davidson and Begley reported on a series of studies where during compassion meditation both expert and novice meditators showed an increase in activity in their insula, "which is essential for activating bodily responses that play a role in feeling another person's suffering and thus in empathy" (2012, p. 219).

Bodies

Mario, a sixty-five-year-old, white, heterosexual car mechanic, wanted to work on dating issues. On my encouragement, Mario started using Headspace, a meditation app that has benefited many of my clients. Having an app puts meditation at your fingertips and provides structure, and using apps is consistent with today's culture. When clients are engaging in a meditation practice, working with them as I am describing is a bit easier, but in-session deep breathing practices and attention to the body also work quite well. I find the practices highlighted in this chapter particularly useful in helping clients with specific Anxiety Problems. Meditation and breathing practices are also extraordinarily helpful with Anxiety management in general, because regular use reduces Anxiety's overall level of influence.

To start this work with Mario, I asked him to come up with an image he found relaxing, something to return to if Anxiety got too big. His

image was lying under a blue sky. It is far from a novel idea in psychotherapy to use relaxing images to provide a safe refuge from Problems in
the conversation, although it is my experience that maintaining breathing and noticing the breath during the conversation usually manage
Anxiety without needing to return to the calming image. Nevertheless, I
asked him to raise a finger if Anxiety got too big, so I could slow the conversation down or bring him back to his relaxing image. White (2004,
2005), in his work on trauma, suggested first bringing forth preferred
stories for the client to provide a foundation of safety; I find images rep-
resenting both the Problem and an anti-Problem experience to be sim-
pler, less cognitive, and more directly related to affect. After Mario and
I engaged in some deep breathing together, I started asking questions
about these dating issues:

1. What's coming up as you are thinking about this?
Mario shared an image of sitting outdoors on a log and putting a match
in a fire; some Anxiety was associated with this image, but he indicated
it was manageable. At the time I thought it was interesting, given his
outdoor "relaxing" image, that the Anxiety image also was located in the
outdoors. It is my experience that the Problem finds some way to worm
its way into preferred places and developments.

2. What's happening in your body as you are picturing this? . . . Where primarily? What might we call this?
Locating the Problem in the body allowed him to get at Anxiety more
directly than when it was in narrative form. He showed me where in the
body it was and called it Tension and Self-Doubt.

3. What image comes up as you are feeling Tension and Self-Doubt in your body?
He described an evil image from the movie *The Watchman*. Note that,
once he located the Problem in his body, he came up with an Anxiety
image very separate from his outdoor relaxing image.

4. What do you think about this happening to you?
I was inviting him to take a position on the Problem. He said, in an

animated way, that he "didn't like it." My experience is that, if the client is connected to the affect related to the Problem, the position the client takes is also more affect filled.

5. Where does "not liking it" leave you?
He said he wanted to "go for it"—in other words, he was ready to keep taking on the Problem.

6. Can you bring it closer?
As we saw with Doug, help in tolerating intense negative affect involves pulling it in, not pushing it out. We worked on doing this with his image, breathing in as he pulled it in, and breathing out as he was "sitting with it."

Toward the end of this part of our session I asked:

7. What was it like for you to do this with me?
As it is often the case, this question brought forth useful experience. He shared that the whole process was uncomfortable for him, because it was something new, and that he always felt uncomfortable when doing new things with others. He had never shared this interpersonal experience with me before; it was easy to imagine the effects of this discomfort on the dating Problem.

He also shared that this process allowed him to take hold of the Problem in a new way, and that he wanted to deal with the discomfort of doing new things with others in our next session. I asked him to pay attention to when this came up between now and the next time I saw him, with particular attention to his body. Sometime after this session he decided to join a group that went on weekend trips and has since become a leader in the group.

Another client of mine, Leslie, was a forty-eight-year-old Asian American, heterosexual engineer who experienced a life-altering medical problem, along with significant difficulties with her son. She was experiencing pressure to get on with her life, from herself, her family, and her doctors. After numerous conversations about this with little effect on her conclusion that she was at fault for being so weak, I asked her to picture what this Problem was like for her. She imagined herself being weighed down by a giant metal ball. I suggested she find a picture of this on the

Internet and keep it in sight during the week. When she returned for her next session, she shared that an epiphany had occurred, a realization that indeed the Problems were massive, and that while they were still there, it was unfair to expect herself to just move forward. The image accomplished what words did not: it brought forth just how difficult things were for her in a way that allowed for new meaning to be made. In addition, looking at the picture brought the affect associated with the Problem more into her body, which allowed us to have a conversation during which she found a way to make the affect more manageable.

Here's example from my work with Chris, a thirty-year-old white, hetero-sexual teacher, that illustrates the usefulness of locating both Problems and developments in the body. Chris was having a crisis of confidence as a teacher, experiencing a good bit of personal failure about not being able to reach some of her students.

J: Where do you feel this guilt and shame?
C: (feels around her body) I guess in my heart.
J: And when that feeling is in your heart, what does it put on your head?
C: I didn't live up to the standards set by my parents . . .
J: (later) You told me that the kids you teach really like your class?
C: Yes, I understand I am loved . . .
J: (interrupting) Can you pick out a time when you really experienced this? I imagine there are many.
C: At the school award ceremony. When my name was called to come forward, the students all began yelling and clapping for me.
J: Can you picture this right now?
C: OK (closes eyes).
J: As you are hearing them clap, what is coming into your body?
C: Love . . . (later) pride . . .
J: Now can you bring the guilt and shame back in? . . . (later) Now the love?

This last piece is a good example of the use of bifurcation questions I discussed in Chapter 3.

I often joke that we Narrative Therapists apparently exist only from the head up—maybe our minds assume our clients are the same way. (My previous ignorance about the importance and richness of possibilities of going to the body cannot be overstated!) Perhaps Narrative Therapy has been influenced by the same mind-body split as has Western psychological discourses. Of course, none of these bodily based ideas is a new thing. Many ancient healing practices have incorporated listening to the body and interpreting its communication as a way to gather more information for healing. Singer (personal communication, 2016) suggested that practices like Reiki, Qigong, and Asana Yoga assume that the healing of the body is central to the healing of the mind. These practices have been taken up in the Westernized world by bodyworkers, dance therapists, and practitioners of alternative medicine but have often been marginalized by dominant psychological discourse. Body-based techniques are on the rise as a result of new research in neuropsychology that can quantify the effects of these practices and help us understand how these practices work. It makes sense, then, that there is an explosion of new psychotherapeutic work containing ideas that reflect a focus on the body and on body-based energies (see, e.g., Ogden, Minton, & Pain, 2006; Ogden, 2009, 2013; Shapiro, 2013; van der Kolk, 2014).

It is widely believed that bodies contain physical manifestations of Problems both past and present and serve as an information device for both clients and therapists. As I have demonstrated, I routinely ask clients to describe where they feel the Problem in their bodies; asking these questions promotes a more mindful relationship with the body and helps me remember to pay attention to my own body as well. As an aside, this kind of mindfulness involves a purposeful focusing of attention (like I described earlier for breathing and for images of the Problem), which is different from the kind of mindfulness involved in just being receptive to whatever comes up. In my personal practice, I use both approaches; in the room with clients, I invite their attention and awareness to images and body sensations. As suggested previously (Zimmerman & Beaudoin, 2015), directing mindfulness to particular indicators (e.g., "This week, notice the Problem at home and work") is an end-of-session intervention used frequently by Narrative Therapists. Now I add, "And also notice where you feel it in your body."

Pat Ogden (2013) suggested that body responses are precursors to action. She offered a number of questions that can be asked, relating bodily based responses to the Problem or to preferred developments (my Narrative language, not hers), for example, What does that feeling in your body want you to do? What conclusions is it encouraging? If the tension could talk, what might it be telling you? Why don't you ask your body how the tension wants you to move, pull in, push out, or push away? What image comes up when you picture this? Of course, these questions won't be useful as purely a cognitive exercise—clients must actually feel the emotions in their bodies.

Body responses to therapist interventions yield useful information, too. If you check in with your client's body periodically, you might get the kind of feedback that will allow you to work on Problems as they manifest in the room; a client's bodily based response is an effect of the past and of what's happening in the session. Ogden went on to suggest that clients may be implicitly inviting, through their physical/nonverbal responses, the therapist to inadvertently support a Problem version (my words). As a process like this emerges, attending less to words and more to bodily based responses and energy flow would put you in a better position to turn down these invitations. Ogden gives an example of a client being frozen and how this invited persistence on her part until she noticed that her responses inadvertently supported the client's frozenness. For me, Frozenness can invite too much talking on my part. Ogden (2013) stated that with some clients possibilities for new actions are restrained because of their previous experience in a similar situation that yielded danger or unresponsiveness. Translating these bodily responses (like frozenness) into words might either reveal preferred directions or yield a name for the Problem that was not accessible through purely verbal means (like with Doug and other clients described in this chapter).

Raymundo, a client you will meet in Chapter 6, got progressively tenser when I began sessions looking for Unique Outcomes (which I did persistently at first). When I finally noticed and checked in with him about his body, he said he felt a tightness in his neck during my questioning; he told me that this process left him feeling unheard. When

I asked him more about this, he said it took him back to experiences with his mother, who pursued her own agenda and not his. I was then able to respond to and acknowledge his bodily based experience and react to his distress in a caring manner that soothed his body (according to his report). In general, continually bringing back what's happening in the room to the client's body, inviting reflection, and then inviting images and/or asking questions has proven extremely useful in my work. I have found it more useful with some clients, instead of inviting verbal descriptions, to start the therapeutic process with what's happening in their body, in the room with me. Under the influence of Ogden's ideas, I have also used the body to amplify emotions with clients who were not very affectively connected. For example, I had a young client jump up and throw up his hands to accentuate the positive emotions he was having difficulty feeling.

What I call Talking-Body involves a group of practices I garnered from my readings that use words or touch to sooth and respond empathically to parts of the body where feelings have been identified. For example, encouraging the client to give the hurting part support from another part (e.g., a hand) provides empathy from one part to another. Additional support can come from using soothing words. Another technique is to put a one hand on your chest, and the other on your stomach, provide mild pressure, and then switch; individuals differ in which direction has the greater effect. Yet another is the Butterfly Hug: put your left hand on your right shoulder, and your right on your left, and then tap alternately. You might attempt these practices yourself and see what effects they have for you.

Try this exercise: breathe, picture the last story you listened to (with a client or a friend), and then ask yourself, was I "in it" as it was being told, or was I readying a response to it? Did I feel the conversation in my body, or was I in my head? Here's a conversation I had with Mickey, a twenty-five-year-old white, gay salesperson, when my body was picking up something different than his words were stating. Mickey sought therapy to deal with the general effects of Anxiety in his life and with being overmanaged at work by his father. In his third session with me, Mickey was "reporting" on his activities at work by rotely reviewing a list of things he had done. Then I asked him:

J: You came in here for Problems affecting your relationship with your dad. What happened when he made his usual appearance at work?

M: (voice rises slightly) It was fine. I think it's ridiculous that he does it.

J: When he does it, what effect does it have on you?

M: Oh, it's overbearing . . . but I am continuing to have success letting it go, so I was able to be pleasant to him.

J: I'd like to hear more about what went into that. But I also wonder, how did you experience it at the time?

M: As we discussed last session (voice rising again), it's like an evaluation . . . but it's fine. It doesn't bother me anymore.

I was hearing Mickey say it was fine, but inside a voice was asking, *then why do I feel so much tension?* (I should have gone to a MOMENT here.) I find that sometimes I don't get the kind of bodily based resonance with clients that allows me to feel their experience; even more crucial, at times like the one described here when the client's body is putting out signals that don't match the words. Sometimes this is due to the influence of the Problem on the client (e.g., Doug), and sometimes it has to do with what's influencing me. In the latter case, I ask myself these questions and try to be mindful of the following:

Where am I looking: up in my head (e.g., thinking about where I should go next, or about what questions to ask), or out at the client (wondering what is going on with the client)?
Am I lost in my client's or my own words? Is there no reflective space between questions, for both myself and the client?

Perhaps the mentality of following a line of questioning has more negative than positive effects in this regard. I really prefer to be able to be in the relationship, present, breathing, going inside and experiencing what is happening between us. Some signs that I am in that state include the following:

I am feeling my body.
I am metabolizing the experience, the relationship (like mothers do with their infants).

There is a flow and I feel it in my body.
I feel connected for stretches, seemingly without effort.

I hope these hints are helpful to you in being able to notice the ways you are participating in your relationships with your clients. We will be addressing the neurobiology of this process in Chapter 5.

Summary: Mind/Body

- *Meditate, meditate, meditate . . .* Meditating continues to help me be more the person I want to be at home and at work. And it's really helped all of my clients who have chosen to make this practice a part of their lives.
- *Breath!* In sessions, I often have clients engage in deep belly breathing before sharing either Problem or Unique Outcome MOMENTS (for ideas about breathing patterns, see Brown & Gerbarg, 2012). The work with Doug and Mario involved long stretches of conversation facilitated by breath awareness. This kind of breathing activates the parasympathetic nervous system*, which counters the agitation (e.g., Doug's panic) generated by activation of the sympathetic nervous system*. Breathing also focuses attention, which activates the mPFC, promoting integration. Breathing this way works well for me, too, before, during, and after sessions.
- *The body is an extraordinarily helpful alternative gateway.* Remember that locating the Problem in the body is not the same thing as locating it in the person's identity or self.
- *Help bypass your clients'* top-down *processes by breathing deep and picturing.* When the conversation involves only words, the client's top-down mind has the most influence. Particularly with clients influenced by a Problem involving the kind of intrapersonal disconnection you saw with Doug, I engage in a process where we together attend to the body's response, come up with an image in relation to that bodily based response, and then scaffold the image by slowly bringing it closer. Only then do words seem useful.
- *There will be energy flow between your self and your body, and between you and others, if you can find ways to open yourself up to it and feel it.*

Bateson (1972) suggested that mind exists between all things, animate or not. The Jedi Yoda (1980) suggested this as well.

- *What about us?* Openness to ourselves increases the likelihood of openness to others and facilitates a decentered position. I believe that co-creation should be not just a practice but a shared experience. For clients to experience resonance with the therapist, the therapist must feel the feelings the client is expressing, not merely engage cognitively.

Now let's catch up with Doug in his next session:

J: How's it going?

D: I've been letting the feelings in, not resisting them. I've been breathing and meditating. I've been more productive.

J: And the wave, the failure wave?

D: I've been letting myself feel it more.

We discussed another Problem MOMENT when he was able to feel and manage his feelings. Then:

D: I now realize how much tenseness I walk around with, how tight I am. I am more alert to this . . . There is this Nut of tension that's bigger or smaller depending on what's happening.

J: Would it be OK if we started to take on this Nut?

Note Doug's development of awareness of the energy flow in his own body. In the next session, Doug reported that things were going better at work (he was able to get work done) and that he had a constructive conversation with his son. In fact, he had made progress with both his children.

J: What do you think enabled you to take these steps?

D: Well, I still have a level of anger and anxiety.

J: The Nut?

D: It has been persistent.

J: I wonder what you have been noticing about the Nut. Have you been picturing it?

D: Expectations, disappointments . . . things should happen faster.

J: How about we breathe for a while (we do so) . . . When you picture the Nut, what is it doing to you?

D: It's making me upset. I can't be effective this way.

J: Can you bring it closer? . . . What's happening in your body?

D: Yes . . . I can feel the tension.

J: I can feel it too (quiet for a bit) . . . You've been most concerned about how the tension, the Nut, affects you around other people, at work, with your kids, yet it seems you have made some steps in this area.

D: I do have a lot of expectations, disappointments . . . with people at work, my kids.

J: Given how the Nut captures this, puts pressure on you and gets you to put it on others . . . how is it, then, that you have been able to manage it better?

D: Well, I have been doing this at home, stopping during the day and breathing and picturing.

J: What do you notice happens when you do this?

D: I become more productive.

J: I know how important that is to you . . . I'm still imagining there is more that you are doing that contributes to these development.

D: I am letting it in.

J: That's big! Can we go back to letting it in, to feeling it right now?

D: Sure . . . (closes his eyes and breathes more deeply)

J: What's happening in your body?

D: I'm experiencing the feelings, the anxiety.

J: (very warmly) OK, I'm with you on this . . . tell me more about what you are feeling, doing.

D: You know for the first time in my life I am working on the ability to process emotions.

J: I imagine that must be uncomfortable at times (he nods) . . . Have you noticed effects of this that you are pleased about?

D: There is less avoidance, more energy . . .

At the end of the session I encouraged him to continue to meditate, breathe, and picture.

In the room, it was clear to me that the tension was really in his body now, as I felt it in a way I hadn't before. You might notice that I showed persistence in inviting him to make meaning about how he managed the Problem and about what contributed to the steps he had taken. I actually asked him a variation of the How did you do it? question three times before he entered into it, instead of giving me a Problem-influenced response. Eventually he told me he had been breathing and picturing, and later that he had been letting the feelings in. Entering into this question allowed us to co-construct agency with respect to those developments and to thicken his relationship to the feelings in his body.

The next session happened about eight weeks later because of his travel schedule:

J: How's it going?

D: This has been the biggest single breakthrough I've ever had psychologically.

J: What do you mean exactly?

D: Well, I still have disappointment, hurt, but I can feel it . . . it's heavy in my body.

J: What difference has it made for you to be able to feel it?

D: There has been a continuing change in my ability to manage stress and anxiety. I stopped taking my anxiety meds. There is no river of anger, no Nut.

J: Let's slow this down a bit . . . Imagine a work scene, and the Nut is threatening.

D: No Nut really, but yesterday at my desk . . .

J: Help me to picture this . . .

Doug describes the scene, filling in the details. Then:

J: Now what are you up to?

D: I'm welcoming the feelings in, experiencing them, interrogating them.

J: Instead of them interrogating you?

D: Yes, I want to know what they mean, what they want.

J: Can you imagine what it might mean for your future to have this new relationship to your feelings?

D: I can deal . . . less avoidance, maybe relate to people better.

J: Have you noticed any effects like that in the present?

D: I mean there is stress, but its *normal*—normal high stress stuff of the job.

J: What about with people?

D: My relationship with my kids has been good, we are communicating . . . I notice that I want to be around people more, even though I am resistant, and there is a fight with Avoidance . . . I have been trying to hang in there (pauses) . . . (looking pained) But I'm not particularly good or warm to my kids or anyone.

J: I do understand from our previous conversations that connection is what you desperately want. We have acknowledged how your pain is a testimony to that, that this is the last frontier of the Problem . . . I'm guessing that if you want that you must have had a taste of it somewhere. I was wondering where you might have experienced something like that in the past.

D: Maybe at summer camp, around middle school (tells me about some boys he had some closeness with) . . . I trusted them.

J: Can we go through a time that stands out for you with them? (Doug goes through a MOMENT) . . . Listening to your experience, I got the impression that it was important for you to be with those boys in a certain way.

D: You know, I recently took some steps to having more integrity with others . . . I told my girlfriend the truth about my financial problems, and then I shared some issues I had with her with a couple of friends.

J: Wow, what was that like for you, to operate with integrity instead of avoidance?

D: Risky . . .

J: So you took some risky steps to be vulnerable?

D: Yes, I can handle this a little better now.

You saw a couple examples how I used bifurcated questions (interrogating them/interrogating yourself, integrity/avoidance). I reflected on Doug's absent but implicit desire for connection ("that connection is what you desperately want . . . your pain is a testimony to that") and then asked a Remembering question ("I was wondering where you might have experienced something like that in the past?"). I then had him enter a MOMENT. I was very aware of wanting to thicken these developments; as you can see, the Problem, having more "neural" strength, tries to reassert itself ("But I'm not particularly good or warm to my kids or anyone"). At this point, however, there is experience behind the New Story. The thing that is invisible to you is that Doug had gotten increasingly warmer with me, and that there was a strong, nonverbal acknowledgment of connection.

I wonder if at this point you can imagine how the practices discussed in this chapter might be especially important to addressing the Problems of today. Is it an accident that meditation and body-oriented interventions have recently gained a great deal of popularity in our culture? Are there real effects of technology that these practices remediate? Chapter 5 describes the important role our right hemispheres play in this turn of events, and how it mediates the way our own neural firing is linked to the activity of other nervous systems.

Chapter 5

Right-Brain to Right-Brain Communication in Narrative Therapy

What we've got here is a failure to communicate.
—Prison guard in *Cool Hand Luke*

Karen is a thirty-five-year-old white, heterosexual human resources worker; Clark, a forty-three-year-old white, heterosexual public relations professional; and Billy is Karen and Clark's fourteen-year-old son:

B: He gets in my face, angry, arguing, he's never wrong . . . he gives me no space. I'm just a mistake.

K: It's difficult being in the middle, but I have to be super careful or he's on me too, judging.

C: It's brutally painful. I have to dig deep to function, and we are struggling as a couple.

J: I'm hoping you will notice some things in the next couple weeks: Clark, the feelings that erupt that get you to pursue Karen; Karen, the effects on you of trying to keep everybody happy; Billy, I get that you have your own therapist and are done trying, that you definitely don't want to be made to talk to your dad . . . that's OK for now.

What makes up the neurobiology of connection and communication? Our middle prefrontal cortex links our own neural firing to the activity of other nervous systems, leading to a process that begins by sensing/feeling what's going on between us and others. Given that nonverbal communication is a primary mode in which emotion is communicated (Neil Carlson, as cited in Siegel, 2012a), some important questions that arise: What allows us to match signals? To experience our own and others' feelings? To make sense of them? To all of a sudden "know" things? What part does this emotional process between people play in creating new narratives?

I like Jim Wilder's (2004) description of right-brain to right-brain communication in his Life Model literature:

> Right-hemisphere-to-right-hemisphere communication occurs when the right brain of a sender puts authentic emotional information on the left side of her face. This expression is perceived by the left side of the retina of both eyes in an observer and sent directly to the observer's right brain. This process is quickly reversed and the right brain of the receiver becomes the sender, putting information about their authentic emotional state on the left side of their face where it is sent back by the same mechanism to the right side of the brain that originally started the process. This communication is so fast the six complete cycles of communication are achieved every second . . . the brains becoming synchronized in their brain chemistry and emotional states. These emotions are amplified each cycle so that a very small emotion can become a strong emotional interaction within a matter of a few seconds. These emotional states are subjectively experienced as though they were produced by the other person. (n.p.)

Mirror Neurons and Intention

Mirror neurons are an important part of our resonance system, which allows us to take in social experience and send responses back out. Giacomo Rizzolatti and Laila Craighero (2004) summarized research in Italy with monkeys, which found that the same sets of neurons were activated when monkeys watched the actions of others as when they performed those actions themselves. Rizzolatti and Craighero then described how this works in humans. Mirror neurons are what prepare us to react in a similar fashion to others. Furthermore, they help us to "understand" the intentions of other people (Iacoboni et al., 2005). We are hardwired to see an act, come to an understanding of the intention behind it (and we believe that this understanding is the truth), and get ready to respond. These neurons respond only to acts of intention or purpose, those with predictable sequences. According to Dan Siegel, "This mirroring is never actually a true replica, we could even dub this a sponge system as we soak up what we see in others and actually make it uniquely our own" (2010a, p. 38). Narrative folks might find this similar to Clifford Geertz's line, "It is the copying that originates" (1886, p. 380) that Michael White was fond of paraphrasing (copying?) in workshops.

Not only is the interpretation of intention hardwired; so is detecting and simulating the internal states of others, leading any number of researchers to posit the involvement of mirror neurons (along with other parts of the brain, including the previously discussed insula) in experiencing empathy. The perceptions generated when witnessing the emotional responses of another affect our internal responses; we feel like we feel what the other does (e.g., when you watch someone drink you feel thirsty; you feel pain at another's pain). This might promote empathy for their feelings, or fear and anger, depending on prior learning and context (e.g., interpretations of intention made in new love relationships are often different from those made in established ones). We believe we have read the other's internal state, and we alter our own behavior and internal state in response. In effect, we make up a story that reflects our view of the intentions behind the other's behavior; however, these interpretations are influenced by our own emotional state. This state is shaped by prior experiences that have occurred both in the relationship and in other relational experiences. This prior learning affects the conclusions about the other and the actions we take accordingly, mediated in effect by a fantasy about the emotions behind the other's behavior, which we are certain is true. We think we feel the other, but we are often really feeling our own emotional response.

Mirror neurons are the neurobiological explanation of what Jerome Bruner (1986, 1990) wrote about when he suggested that intention affects interpretation. Bruner suggested that if someone's responses don't fit with what we think should happen based on social expectations, we will interpret the intention behind it accordingly. Expectations are shaped both by common and personally idiosyncratic social experiences and by the emotions that all of these kinds of experiences bring with them. Bruner's explanation was predominantly a cognitive/canonical one; consistent with modern neurobiology, mine is more of an emotional one. From this point of view, emotions influence the knowledge, skills, behavioral responses, and interpretations we bring (or don't bring) to bear on a situation. Perhaps you can see how inseparable Bruner's land-scapes of action and consciousness are; motor action is influenced by experience, by these interpretations made by our minds.

In the next session with Karen and Clark:

C: Billy actually talked to me for the first time in weeks . . . I've gone easy on him. Most of our stresses revolve around Billy, but Karen responds to these issues without listening to me. I want to slow things down; *she's not interested.* I want to stay focused on a goal, but it seems to wear Karen out.

J: What does this "goal pursuit" look like? How does it have you act-ing toward Karen?

C: Karen says I push too hard.

J: What effect does this seem to have on Karen?

C: She disappears.

J: And then on you?

C: It sets me off . . . eventually I stop reaching out and do my own thing.

J: What's it like for you as a person when you feel that Karen won't work with you?

C: I feel worthless; we can have very good discussions at times . . .

K: But my emotions spiral. I feel so much anxiety . . . I'm so small. It's the tone he uses.

J: What does that put in your head about Clark?

K: He has so many harsh expectations . . . *I feel judged, attacked . . . he's so disappointed in me*, I get no approval for anything.

J: When those emotions overtake you, how do they have you responding to Clark?

K: I pull back, sometimes I yell and then leave the room.

J: Have you always experienced Clark's tone this way?

K: Early in our relationship *I felt valued by him . . . he wanted to care for me.*

Later:

J: I'm hoping that in the next couple of weeks, Karen, you can notice "Pushing" or "Pulling Back" taking over you with Clark, and what's happening in your body at that time.

To illustrate how mirror neurons work, in this dialogue I have highlighted the interpretations being made by each member of the couple about the conclusions and intentions of the other. In the room I sensed how much Fear was dividing this couple, influencing how they were currently reading and responding to each other. Neither seemed to feel particularly safe; Karen showed this more directly, while Clark, in a "nice" way, justified his attempts to get Karen to do things the way he wanted. If, as Rhonda Goldman and Leslie Greenberg (2013) have suggested, affect regulation* (i.e., affect management) is the core motive of attachment*, then it is easy to see why each is moving away from the other. As an overall effect of their current interactions, their emotions are getting less manageable; consequently, their right brains are taking over management of the situation from their left. Note also how I attempted to make the negative cycle the Problem (Clark pushing, Karen pulling back), how the type of reaction is the opposite of what you would expect gender-wise, and how these responses are generated by emotional states (Karen: Clark "sets me off" / "so much anxiety").

Right and Left Brains

Chapter 2 began the discussion of the important differences between right and left brains. What about those right brains? They develop early in utero and are fast acting, are activated by images and stories (not rhetoric or information), and generally mediate the emotional aspects of our lives. Right brains are also where autobiographical memories are stored (i.e., landscape of consciousness), holding representations of the emotional states associated with events we have experienced. A picture of the internal world of the self and others resides in the right brain. Right-hemisphere arousal is related to negative affect and withdrawal, including from others (shyness is seen as excessive reactivity of the right brain and is likely genetic). For example, babies who cry more show more right-hemisphere activation (Siegel, 2012a).

In contrast, the left brain develops later, is slow acting, is text activated, and is the more interpretive, conclusion-generating area of the brain. It is the landscape of action; routine details are pieced together to help us move forward. Left-hemisphere arousal is related to positive affect and is approach oriented. However, the left brain can become rigid and shape us in a narrow direction. We have known for some time that this rigidity can be addressed by more integration with the right brain, as more emotionality can open up forward rigid movement. As you saw with Doug, pictures and imagery will bring in the right brain which facilitates experiencing things closer to how they actually are.

Why are most people right-handed? Because of cross-dominance, the right hand activates the left brain, which mediates our efforts to "grasp" or navigate the world (McGilchrist, 2013). The left brain chooses what to attend to, helping us make sense of the world but inevitably altering it. The left brain is quite certain of its conclusions but operates with a limited view. It uses a single solution based on what it decides is the best fit and stays focused on pursuing it, emphasizing strategy over experiencing. However, in this process, it blindly fills in information to complete the picture that we are unaware it is making up. In effect, we experience a re-presented version, a useful fiction. In the Narrative Therapy world, for example, we have long suggested that Problem stories include only some of the experiences of a person's life—those that don't fit are left out.

This left-brain process and its reliance on language narrows the field, resulting in an overreliance on explicit reasoning, without any perspective of the big picture and no possibility for novel information. This is in contrast to the right brain, which has the "big picture" and tends to spread out and generate a matrix of alternatives—things come into focus as a whole. The left brain's linear process puts things together one by one, viewing still frames, seeing only parts and categories. The left brain even sees the body as parts. The right brain sees things in context, more like a movie, and therefore appreciates uniqueness. Despite the left brain's lack of context, seeing the world through the left brain leaves us with a superior, know-it-all perspective, unaware of our limited vision. The left brain views the world as something we can use; this involves operating only in relation to ourselves, not others. Does this sound familiar in any way? To bring us back to the context of therapy, I keep raising the dilemma of therapists thinking primarily in terms of questions, categories of responses, or theory, instead of attending to clients, staying plugged into and in touch with them—perhaps doing so would represent the big picture in any interpersonal context.

In the next session with Karen and Clark:

K: I was able to notice, after the fact, what happened in my body before pulling back.

J: Can you describe it to me?

K: So aroused . . .

J: Like it was triggered?

K: So unbearable . . . in my core, like I was in a fight for my personhood.

J: I'm getting a sense of danger . . . is that right?

K: Yes!

J: Have you felt anything like this before?

K: Yes. Starting at a very early age, I was treated for a polio-like problem . . . so much shame . . . so Small!

J: Were you tempted to share this with Clark?

K: I wanted to. I've told him about this some in the past . . .

J: What made that possible in the past?

K: I felt safe.

J: Can you picture that now? Can you call up that memory?

K: Yes. There was trust, closeness, connection . . . I miss it.

J: Does remembering this make any difference to the relationship?

K: *Maybe these reactions of his aren't so personal . . .*

J: That seems like an important conclusion to me . . . does it to you? How might that conclusion affect what you hear from Clark in the future?

K: That his responses don't necessarily always reflect how he feels about me.

J: I was also wondering if noticing your own reactions was helpful to you in supporting the relationship.

K: I was able to stay in conversation longer . . . I was able to see that Clark and Billy are both hurting, that I need to look out more for their relationship.

J: I'm guessing that this picture of you works better for you than the Small picture?

K: Yes, I feel so much more grown up.

J: I'm hoping you will continue to notice what happens when Small-ness enters your body and gets you to Pull Back, how it takes you away from the grown-up feeling you want and allows Smallness to get what it wants.

J: (turning to Clark) And you, Clark?

C: Billy told me that he didn't like me, and Karen didn't say any-thing . . . I felt out of control and retreated.

J: What about the Push thing?

C: I'm not really sure the Push thing is what it is . . . I did notice Karen not following through, but we were able to talk about it.

J: What do you think contributed to this ability to talk about it, as opposed to getting into the pattern we discussed last time?

C: Karen talked to me instead of giving me feedback on my behav-ior . . . (Clark seemed more angry about the feedback than happy with Karen for talking about it with him instead of giving feed-back or Pulling Back.)

J: Can you picture a time when you felt you were getting this feed-back response?

C: Oh yes . . .

J: Close your eyes and picture . . . what's happening in your body?

C: Very bad feelings . . .

J: And what responses were the bad feelings getting you to make?

C: Well, there was some impatience, maybe some abruptness.

J: How else were the feelings getting you to treat Karen?

C: *I guess I was pushing my point of view* . . . she needs to be willing to include me.

J: These type of bad feelings, have you experienced them before?

C: Well, my father was critical . . .

J: How did that affect your view of yourself?

C: It didn't make me feel amazing. Thankfully I found some friends later in life where I got feedback that I was kind and sensitive. That fixed the problem.

I spent some time asking Clark some Re-membering questions about this to thicken this picture of him. And then:

J: Was there a time when you saw yourself through Karen's eyes in the same way you saw yourself through your friends' eyes?

C: Early in the relationship.

J: How would you describe the look in her eyes then?

C: An adored gaze.

J: When you experienced this adored gaze, what was that like for you?

C: I felt safe . . .

In this session I was able to begin to touch on some of the underlying emotions behind the Push–Pull Back cycle. There was clearly much more there, but I wanted to take it slow to keep it safe. (The all important feeling safe issue is addressed in Chapter 6.) In general, I was following their experiences carefully, and as it often does, this process seemed to open the door to reflections, to generating some of their own new conclusions.

I find that following and letting myself experience my client's experience and then responding with a question (or even a comment) generated by my experience of their experience often has this effect—"jumping" to a question is a poor substitute for careful following. Creating experience, bringing forth their affective experience, brings in the right brain more, which allows them to have a bigger picture than the left brain's "just deal with what is in front of me" strategy. When the affective information is brought in and a bigger picture is created, the left brain then puts together a new story.

With Karen, in the beginning of the sequence I reflected a sense of danger to her as I was feeling it. When Karen said, "I was in a fight for my personhood," it suggested to me that more here was involved than just what was happening with Clark. With Clark, when he "resisted" the Pushing identified in our last session, I just kept following him until he came back to it himself. Clark basically told me that the Problem related to his dad was fixed, although I thought his phrase, "It didn't make me feel amazing" was interesting. It sure seemed that something was influencing his responses to Karen, leading him to act in ways that were clearly not preferred. Perhaps both of their emotional responses were being fueled by feelings of life threat*, prompting their right brains to have more influence over their reactions. Nevertheless, under the influence of remembered past moments, I was able to bring forth positive present-day feelings, which, when shared with me, generated some new conclusions and possibilities.

Ian McGilchrist, in his 2009 book *The Master and the Emissary*, suggested that our brains are supposed to work with the right as the master and the left as the emissary, but the effects of technology appear to be upsetting this balance. He offered the following vision of a left-brain-dominated future: increasing specialization and technicalizing of knowledge, increased bureaucratization, an inability to see the big picture, a focus on quantity and efficiency at the expense of quality, a valuing of technology over human interaction, a lack of respect for judgment and skill acquired through experience, and a devaluing of the unique, the personal, and the individual. In addition, skills would be reduced to algorithmic procedures that could be drawn up and even, if necessary, regulated by administrators. Fewer people would find themselves doing work involving contact with anything in the real "lived" world, and technology would flourish as an expression of the left hemisphere's desire to manipulate and control the world for its own pleasure.

As you can see, our world has already become very much this way. A therapy that would remediate the effects of this direction would activate the right brain and promote more mindful attention to one's inner life and emotions, one's body, and one's connection to others. As an example that reflects the effects of these cultural developments, Sara Konrath, Edward O'Brien, and Courtney Hsing (2011) found that college students' empathy scores have dropped and hypothesized that this was an effect of less direct visual contact with others due to use of electronic media; this further suggests that an emphasis on right-brain therapeutic practices might be in order. Back in the day, when we moved from a society where physical activity was the rule to one where many had more sedentary lives, people began practicing physical exercise. Now this is considered a given in our lives. Based on what I have been just reviewing, might we soon be at the point culturally where we will all practice mind exercises, to give us time to reflect, to get a sense of ourselves and others, to bring our right brains online? Indeed, have we gotten to the point where, as Allen Schore (2012) suggested, straightforward cognitive approaches seem to be unhelpful? Schore also noted that low stress is handled by the left brain and higher stress by the right. I return to this in Chapter 6.

The right brain is meant to have precedence because it synthesizes both brains into a whole. While the left brain provides specific detail, we need the right brain's influence to get the overall gist of things (in other words, context versus text). As an interesting example, McGilchrist (2013) stated that birds eat with the right eye (therefore using the left brain to grasp the world) and use the left eye to look out for predators (right brain). Going back to Rick Hanson's (2013) point, the bigger picture is to have lunch, not be lunch.

Experience/Reflect

The bigger picture in this book is that activating the right brain is done by creating affective experience. Only then might we usefully invite observing, reflecting, and "new" narrating. In a sense, at any point in time our reflections are from a historian's "distance," that is, from a particular point of view, and as we have just learned, the left brain tends to take a view that is potentially useful but isn't necessarily the whole truth. Ultimately, all history appears to be like that: some sort of experience processed through the left brain, a (hopefully) useful fiction. But clients come to see us because their fictions are not useful—they are not leading to actions or points of view that are having good effects. As observing circuits allow for mental time travel, integrating the past, present, and likely future, we need to be sure our clients have access to all the possible information necessary for creating new narratives. Louis Cozolino (2016) pointed out that we organize experience through mental time travel because it reduces anxiety and gives us a sense of control. Because observing circuits are mediated by the prefrontal cortex, it would be ideal to have information from both sides of the brain.

We need to be able to differentiate observation from experience, historical reflection from narrative construction, in other words, to come up with a story that is based more in emotional experience. Posttraumatic stress disorder is an interesting example: those influenced by it seem to have very little direct access to right-brain information. Folks given this label tend to be unaware of emotional responses and have difficulty describing them (Frewen et al., as cited in Lanius, Bluhm, & Frewen, 2013). They get lower scores on emotional awareness scales. They show less activation in the (dorsomedial) prefrontal cortex on a functional magnetic resonance image when presented with positive or negative scripts, and showed much less activation in the prefrontal cortex than, for example, those engaging in mindful observing (Lanius et al., 2013). Reflection, and ultimately narration, for those labeled with a posttraumatic stress disorder comes without direct access to their feelings.

Back to Karen and Clark—in the next session, after reviewing the last session with them:

J: I wonder what you have been noticing along these lines during the last couple of weeks.

C: I've been observing, and practicing.

J: What has stood out for you?

C: I've experienced a sweeter attitude coming from Karen.

J: What effect does that have on you?

C: I'm getting something back. I can see it's the way we can be.

J: And in terms of how you respond to Karen?

C: I'm more playful.

J: And the relationship?

C: We are closer. It has a more intimate feel.

J: I'm wondering what else you might be doing to support the relationship?

C: I'm watching Pushing . . .

J: What made you decide to attend to that?

C: I don't want to hurt Karen, but there is still stuff I am holding onto, that I feel trepidation about discussing.

J: I'm curious about that . . . whenever you are ready . . .

But Clark clearly wasn't ready, so we had a discussion instead about the values he holds that stand against him hurting Karen. Later we addressed Karen's issues:

K: I'm listening more . . . and I'm nicer to Clark.

J: What would you call the thing that makes this difficult?

K: Assumptions.

J: It seems like you are moving away from these, is that right?

K: Yes, I feel more connected, and I have a desire to connect.

J: Can you take me through a MOMENT when you felt that way?

K: (goes through MOMENT) . . . playful, engaged, connected . . .

J: What can you now see yourself doing as a result of this experience?

K: (still in the MOMENT) Being proactively open.

J: Is this a familiar feeling to you at all?

K: Like in the past.

J: Like how?

K: Peaceful, calm, trusting.

J: Are you still picturing this?

K: Yes . . .

J: The experience you are having right now is different than how you have been feeling recently?

K: Yes. I felt only Clark's disappointment . . . I wrapped a steel core around myself.

J: But now?

K: Acceptance for who I am (smiling).

The Push–Pull Back cycle was starting to be pushed aside for a growing influence cycle of Playful-Open. With Karen I was able to connect this alternative cycle with past moments from their relationship. They were beginning to have interactions that provided validation for each other, which increased the feelings of safety in the relationship and was having positive effects on the perceptions they hold of each other and of themselves. Both were also becoming increasingly more aware of what they do to participate in the Problem cycle. When I asked Clark, "I'm wondering what else you might be doing to support the relationship," perhaps my right brain was picking something up ("I'm watching Pushing"). Karen's use of the metaphor of wrapping "a steel core around her," and the nonverbal communication that went with it, continued to communicate to me that there was a lot of pain sitting inside her. And Clark was "holding onto stuff."

Nonverbal Communication of Experience: Interpersonal Process

Right-brain to right-brain communication has huge implications for how we all connect, because much of what comprises our transactions with others occurs in this manner. EEG studies of reciprocal communication document an interbrain communication of right-brain regions in both interacting partners (Dumas et al., as cited in Schore, 2012). We register constant messages from others at a speed not possible with conscious choice, messages mediated by tone, tempo, rhythm, and body language. These constant right-brain message communications shape our relational expectations more than do cognitive communications. When we are with others, we frequently have intuitions or hunches or contemplate a sudden shift in direction. Schore (2012) suggested that this is not conceptual exercise but an effect of what we are picking up experientially from the other person or from encountering a scenario familiar to us. This information is retrieved by the right brain and incorporated in our reasoning processes. The implication of this, for Schore, is that psychotherapy may be more of a right-brain to right-brain affair.

In discussing right-brain to right-brain communication, we are talking about something that is happening between all of us, all of the time. In the therapy world, these nonverbal, prosodic, positional communications between client and therapist are referred to as *interpersonal process*. This has not been a point of reference in Narrative Therapy, in which the client's verbal descriptions and conscious purpose have traditionally been the focus. Back in the mid-1980s and early 1990s, with concern for moderating the power imbalances constructed between therapist and client in traditionally oriented psychotherapies, this focus made sense. We wanted to privilege the experience of the client and stay away from therapists making process interpretations that the client, given the power differential, would be strongly invited to believe were true. Nevertheless, Narrative Therapy directions aside, two conversations are always taking place: the one where something is being told, and the process one between limbic systems, taken in by the left ear, and sent to the right brain (Ross Buck, as cited in Schore, 2011). The autonomic nervous system* then reacts to these perceptual stimuli, which may never enter consciousness, and triggers a central nervous system response. Schore (2011) suggested that something like an interpersonal sea is created and experienced viscerally and that what happens between people might be called sharing versions or identities. In response to the signals of whomever we are interacting with, we both match versions and adjust our social attention, stimulation, and accelerating arousal. This matching reflects our understanding of which version of ourselves is responsive to that version of the other (a quid pro quo). Perception of a switch to an unexpected version involves voices, faces, gestures, smells, and pheromones (Brancucci et al., as cited in Schore, 2011). Philip Bromberg (2011) posited that this is a relational process, a personal interaction between the mind of the individual and whoever and whatever is out there. But what happens when the implicit contract to be a certain way to each other is broken? Can we be responsive to this switch and remain attuned to the other? Because it occurs suddenly and on a visceral level, do we even feel safe enough to respond while still in a preferred version, without necessarily understanding what has happened cognitively? (I return to this challenge of safety in Chapter 6.)

These questions are important when discussing shifting interactions with our clients. It would be useful to notice when a change has occurred between the version of ourselves and the version of our client and address it; this recognition may not happen until after the session is over and so could become a topic for the next time. A related process-level concern might be how the Problem may be impacting the therapeutic relationship, how it is affecting both members and the way we are interacting with each other. These concerns might lead to the question of how our clients are experiencing themselves in their relationship with us: "What's it like for you to be talking about this with me?" Addressing this can be thought of as an in-session MOMENT, either a Problem one or one that represents a unique outcome. These MOMENTS can then be linked to MOMENTS in a person's life—past, present, or future. (I return to this "what's it like" question in Chapter 6 as well.)

A sudden change in topic (either by the client or by the therapist) or a felt experience of a change in energy may indicate that something has indeed happened. I know that, for me, if the emotional contact exceeds my comfort level, I run the risk of telling a story from my personal experience, often a humorous one, to decrease the emotional arousal in the room. Maybe I'll do a quick didactic lesson in neurobiology. If the energy gets too low, I feel sleepy and my mind wanders. In therapy, it is helpful to be attuned to these fluctuating moment-to-moment experiences of what it is like to be with our clients and for our clients to be with us—to reiterate, this is not a cognitive affair. Perhaps, in our Narrative Therapy work, we (nonconsciously) "feel" shifts in the room and out pops a particular question.

In the next session with Karen and Clark:

C: (smiling) Billy is back responding to me, being my son . . . this is great!

J: I am so happy for you! What does this mean for your relationship with Karen?

C: We can go back to sharing being parents again. It's novel that we can talk about Billy. I've been sad and angry about being shut out, for Karen to be the only one dealing with Billy. I felt desperate.

J: A familiar desperation?

C: Like with my dad? I've been over that for some time . . .

J: And you, Karen?

K: Yes, it's been a good couple of weeks. Clark has continued being playful with me like he used to be, and I have been responsive. I've been giving lots of warm fuzzies.

C: She has been really sweet with me lately.

J: What do you remember about Karen when she treats you that way? What do you know about the relationship?

C: That she wants me in her life, that the relationship is loving.

J: Can you both take me through a MOMENT that illustrates what was happening in the relationship that means so much to you?

K: (instantly sitting back and looking up) On the couch, watching TV, holding each other, being loving like we used to be . . . maybe he does value me, does want to care for me.

Reading this dialogue, I realize that with Clark, despite his being quite clear that he felt he had worked through the issues with his dad, I am quick to jump into the question: "A familiar desperation?" Why was that? From the emotions I was receiving in my body, it did not seem likely that these issues were worked through (a right-brain to right-brain communication?), but I also understand that, if he's not comfortable going there, I need to more carefully scaffold my responses to him. I could have started with, "Tell me more about this desperation," and proceeded slowly from there. Instead I jumped to the question and then switched to Karen, perhaps frustrated with his response. Something was up in my reactions to Clark. I don't like men who are verbally pushy with their wives, but it seemed more than just that. In the next session:

C: Billy continues to move in a good direction. I've been quiet, pay-ing attention . . .

J: And with Karen?

C: There has been a nicer feeling and more warmth of late, but I would still like to engage more. I have been working on being that super-good person.

J: Can you share a MOMENT here?

C: (he doesn't) I've been feeling and acting more generous. I do feel it . . .

J: But . . . (sensing a but)

C: (feeling safer now) There has been an absence of intimacy, of closeness. I feel I carry most of the burden, which I am happy to do, but I'd like a little more acknowledgment . . . (looks sad)

J: Tell me more about this Lack of Acknowledgment . . .

C: Yes, a Loss . . .

J: Is this Loss all of a sudden, recent?

C: I have been feeling this way for some time . . . I'm not seen or understood.

K: I feel like I give him acknowledgment. *He* just doesn't get it. Then he demands it. Here comes Judgment . . . I feel smaller, like in the past. I'm not lovable . . . then the steel barrier comes out. (looks angry)

J: So when this happens the painful stuff starts to take over . . .

K: (interrupting) But when he shares his feelings about this in a heartfelt manner, I can respond to it differently.

J: And the warm fuzzies you said you were interested in showing him the last time?

K: I have continued to put them out there.

J: Help me to picture this, let's find a MOMENT . . .

Goldman and Greenberg (2013) suggested that dominance displays, such as bossy or nagging behavior, represent an attempt to define reality, toward an end of covering up or not allowing vulnerability. You have seen how this fits for Clark; I do a better job of following him in this conversation. You can see the different effects on Karen when he comes from a demanding place versus a more vulnerable one. If I can help bring the uncomfortable affect into his body, then he won't have to manage it by bringing forth a pushier version of himself. Karen's use of the Small metaphor appears to relate nicely to her early-life experience of being literally smaller. How can I use my relationship with them to bring the affect forth and trigger the formation of new narratives?

Putting the Narrative in Narrative Therapy

Communication between therapist and client takes on greater importance when considering outcome research suggesting that relationship factors (i.e., nonverbal process experiences) account for most of the variance in psychotherapy. In effect, what gets done in therapy is an expression of experiences in relationship. From this point of view, new meaning or insight occurs in interactions and is a reorganization of the meaning of present experience. In other words, insight emerges from (psychological) interaction—it is a consequence of change, not a cause of it (Bromberg, 2011).

White (2011) was clear that, if client and therapist are in process (he didn't use that word), the therapist would also be changed. When change does occur, individually, we experience a sense of expansion and positive affect, an aliveness. On a dyadic level, we experience a feeling of connection. If either of these kinds of experiences is absent, it is likely that no new meaning has been made.

According to Edward Tronick (2009), meaning is biopsychosocially polymorphic; for example, emotions have meaning. Meaning is usually discussed as linguistic, symbolic, or abstract, but it is also bodily based (physiological), behavioral, and emotional. For infants, meaning is sensorimotor: it's made without language. Tronick believes that this is the foundational form of sense making, as infants are emotional-meaning-making devices. Over time, emotions remain the foremost elements of meaning, despite being internally created in new emergent forms (e.g., infants don't have shame). Narrative meaning tends to colonize experience; it is never equivalent to the flow of meanings experienced. (Perhaps the breathing and meditation practices described in Chapter 4 can get us closer to this flow.) While in this flow, different narrative meanings both emerge and are incorporated into a state of consciousness over time. The specific construction of these narrative meanings is influenced by the discourses prominent in our lives.

To put our discussion in a Narrative Therapy context, it is not just questions that have an effect, but questions that are affect-filled and experienced in a relationship context. Creating new meaning is not primarily a cognitive process; what's important is the moment-to-moment relational experience. The integration of experience into larger units of meaning has real effects on meaning making in the moment. Yet, this is not the whole story.

Bromberg (2011) suggested that in therapy, to shift narrative meaning, a relational context must be constructed that includes the realities of both therapist and client, and that as therapists we are not trying to helpfully and logically extract a person's reality and replace it with a better one, *even if it's a reality ferreted out from the client's own alternative experiences.* Instead, he suggested that, ideally, we are co-constructing (my words) an experience that is perceivably different from the client's narrative memory. For Bromberg, something happens between the client's unstoried affect and the therapist's, and we can feel it. A moment such as this can have the effect of changing narratives.

Several sessions later with Karen and Clark, things had generally continued to move in a good direction, with me engaging them in a relationship Reauthoring process, with some secondary content issues discussed.

I didn't know it then, but there would be, as Michael White used to joke, an "Is there a therapist in the room?" MOMENT in this session. Karen and Clark came to the session looking as angry and distant as I had seen them in some time. They told me they had a church meeting about Billy's behavior, where from Clark's perspective Karen took over (her anxiety gets her to take over and react nonrelationally). Clark felt shut out, and he reacted strongly to this (his anxiety gets him to put pressure on her). Karen felt judged, and so up went her steel barrier, which seemed to invite Clark to push more (the old pattern), and both disconnected. Neither could handle the switch back into versions of the other that had such bad effects on each of them. Neither could I, it seemed:

K: No shared understanding, all things taken the wrong way, no sympathy or empathy for each other . . .

C: She makes this declarative comment "I think" instead of framing it as an opinion in a team process, which would reflect more of a "we" . . . she always does this.

K: I just say it that way. You know that I mean, "This is my opinion, what's yours." I believe that we . . .

C: Do I? Words are important, they mean something. We are not a team . . .

J: (this had been building for me) What makes them hard to see as just words?

C: I travel in a word world. They are not unimportant.

J: (the tension building) Why can't you see them as just words for Karen, words that have little meaning for the relationship?

This was not a happy ending to the session for any of us. I could have more usefully said to Clark, "Tell me more about the importance of these particular words to you," or "I can see how important these words are to you," or "What experiences have you had that make the emphasis on team so important?"; or, to both: "It seems as if the old pattern has taken over— what's that been like for your relationship?" Why wasn't I able to be more skillful here? Partly I was reacting to the anger and tension in the room; it also felt to me that Clark was verbally bullying Karen. My reaction to the effect of all this on me was to take away my perspective, to "forget" that Karen's withdrawal from a relational position to a self position to deal with the anxiety she was feeling about Billy had real effects for Clark. Eventually, I realized how triggered I was, that Clark reminded me of how my father used to position himself—although he was not as nice about it as Clark. This is the "unstoried affect" that Bromberg referred to—how will we recover from this, what is important here, and what effects will this have on all the relationships?

In his concept of enactments, Bromberg (2011) used the idea of a "safe surprise" that occurs in an authentic experiential moment between client and therapist, when both share their own experience of something that has occurred between them, and from this difference emerges new meaning. Bromberg suggested these enactments change opinions, that something happening *between* people creates change. (From a Narrative Therapy perspective, reflecting teams create such an experience between the group members and the client; W. Lax, personal communication, 2014.)

Here is an example with Frank, a client who was dealing with issues related to developmental trauma. Our time for his session had just run out, and when Frank said, "I guess its time for me to go," I said, strongly, "I'm not ready for you to leave"—this just popped out of my mouth. At the beginning of the next session:

> F: Last time was the best session I ever had with a therapist.
> J: How come?
> F: Your asking me not to leave . . . I had an epiphany, about not taking things so personally. I had three opportunities to be triggered and wasn't.

And in the next session with Karen and Clark:

> J: I want to start with an apology to you, Clark. I feel I pressed you on the words thing instead of appreciating its importance to you. It must feel really terrible to you when she starts that way.
> C: I since made a decision not to press Karen anymore, to be more accepting, to believe she means well. I want her to feel less challenged . . . (crying) *I don't want to hurt her . . .*
> K: I have felt so bad and angry the last two weeks, so not fortified, *but now I am so moved by Clark's feelings for me, so sustained . . .*
> J: What does it mean to you to feel the way Clark feels about you?
> K: It means so much to me. It means we can have a good future, can have talks together. I don't want to block Clark from Billy!

At the start of the session I made an attempt to repair* the relationship. However, it seems that whatever happened between me and Clark opened the door for new meaning for him. Clark became more in touch with the effects of the Problem on Karen, and his response created new emotional meaning for her that shifted her view of him and the relationship.

In my experience, we therapists can count on having times when we are not attuned or having our response shaped by our own implicit affect—

this is inevitable and can have real effects on the relationship. I agree with Bromberg (2011): it is certainly my experience that, if processed, these can be turning points in the work. Bromberg suggested that even ordinary events such as running late or being ill might provoke such a process. I give an example of that sort of thing in Chapter 6.

Goldman and Greenberg (2013) suggested that it is the display of vulnerable emotions that has a meaningful effect on the other person. You can see the impact of Clark's heartfelt display of emotions on Karen. As far as Clark's promise not to press Karen anymore, however, I experienced an interesting dilemma. Although I supported Clark's conscious purpose not to hurt Karen, I also believed that in certain circumstances he would be too triggered to be able to hold on to that purpose. In those circumstances, there would be too much internal stress, his right brain would take over, and he would become reactive. Until that implicit affect is addressed, he runs the risk of that affect influencing him. You get a glimpse of this in his inability to give an unqualified validating response to Karen in some of the previous sessions.

Summary: Right-Brain to Right-Brain Communication

- *Therapy = new emotional experience in the context of a relationship.*
- Right brain first—it's the master. Then invite the left brain to do its thing and make up a story—affective experience, then meaning. *Only new emotional experiences change meaning.*
- Like Dorothy, *follow, follow, follow, follow*; try to stay with what's emergent. This includes sudden narrative departures, which can be noticed and processed (or not, depending on what you are experiencing about your client's experience). Your own departures are meaningful as well!
- Explore, experience, reflect, and then externalize. Let the process unfold before using Narrative practices to build stories, Problem or otherwise. Questions can create or invite interpersonal experience, but they may not; process discussions always do.
- Experience is always occurring between you and the client. Meta-process it with "experience of experience" questions: What was

the client's experience of talking about that with you? What's it like for the client to have you feeling what they feel? What's it like to receive caring responses? Ask about the client's story about you as a therapist or person. Given my greater attention to interpersonal process, I pay more attention to how I am presenting myself to clients (e.g., I am conscious of smiling now). Potentially, all is available to process, including the relationship and the overall experience of the session. Lastly, bring forth the conclusions about "intentions" that clients are making, about yours and about others in their lives. These conclusions can be situated as an effect of the Problem. This includes their conclusions about your intentions and yours about theirs.

- Don't be afraid to let "stuff" happen between you and your client; it is inevitable. Process it, feel it, and deal with the fallout.
- *When tempted to be didactic, go to others' experience.*

During the next session with Karen and Clark:

K: It's been a better two weeks. There were things that could have gone bad but didn't. No disconnections.

J: Could you pick a MOMENT like that, when things could have gone wrong but didn't, so we could go through it?

Karen told a story about Billy wanting to go to a game at school, and she volunteered to go with him, as usual, given the issues with Billy and Clark. Clark felt shut out and reacted angrily, saying something she experienced as diminishing. I interrupted:

J: Hold on . . . as you are picturing this, what are you noticing yourself doing? How did you manage not to disconnect?

K: I'm not sure. I told Clark how I felt about his comments . . .

J: Even in the face of his anger? How did you hang in there?

K: Somehow it felt less threatening than in the past.

J: Less threatening . . . how were you able to catch it at the time, to not let the steel barrier overtake you?

K: Well, it was sort of conscious. I didn't react.

J: That must have been difficult for you, to handle those feelings.

K: I wasn't made smaller. It didn't feel as visceral.

J: I guess I'm wondering what Clark might have done to contribute to that?

K: He did listen to me, to my experience.

J: What was that like?

K: Validating.

J: Validating . . . could you go back to picturing this? What was in your body at the time?

K: A calmness, peace.

J: I'm wondering what that peace enabled you to do. Maybe make it easier for him?

K: I think I was able to get his being upset.

J: Do I have this right—you were able to hold on to yourself like that and then respond to Clark's feelings instead?

K: It was a really good feeling to acknowledge him, his dignity. (Clark's smiling)

J: Do you see this as a step for you, to share your feelings, to hear his?

K: It didn't make me crazy.

J: How is it different than if the steel barrier came up instead?

K: I'd be shut down, angry (clenching her hands as she said this). I'd have to fortify myself.

J: I noticed you clenching your hands . . . what . . .

K: Yes . . . that's it . . .

J: The craziness . . .

K: Yes . . .

J: As you are feeling it, clenching your hands, what does that bring up? Is that the past craziness we talked about? (Karen nods) Can you perhaps share a MOMENT from the past?

K: There were so many (looking upset).

J: Maybe a marquee experience (warmly smiling, mildly joking).

K: (smiling but still looking tense, thinking) Well, there's that one . . . no, . . . here's one, maybe . . . (she tells a story of shame, feeling Small, irrelevant, having little dignity).

J: How do you think that experience is affecting you today?

K: Really insecure . . .

J: It seems like it's painful to talk about this. What's it like for you?

K: I feel such sadness, about being different from others, having to hide.

J: Yes. Is it hard to hold all that sadness.

K: It is uncomfortable.

J: You look ready to be done with this for now. Tell me one more thing. In light of the story you just shared with me, I'm thinking again about the recent development you shared with me earlier, when you were able to hold on to your dignity and to acknowledge Clark's. What that might mean about you?

K: (crying) Maybe I'm not so Small.

J: Can you share with me some MOMENTS when you didn't feel Small?

Karen talked about some of her MOMENTS. Later the discussion turned to Clark:

J: Clark, what was it like for you to witness my conversation with Karen?

C: I really felt her pain. I love her so much (crying).

J: As you are feeling her pain, I'm wondering about your own.

C: (still upset looking) I never got validation from my dad, not much self worth. I didn't believe in myself (crying again) . . . Later I got validation from some people who took me in.

Picking a MOMENT when things could have gone wrong but didn't has you working at the edge of clients' window of tolerance*. Often change begins at this point, as they are starting to manage their arousal, and this has real effects for them and for the others around them. (I discuss this further in Chapter 6.) Working with the arousal in a MOMENT keeps affect in a client's body, and allows for the affect to be experienced in the context of the client's relationship with you. It is then important to bring forth the client's skills and knowledge in managing arousal. In addition, in the situation Karen described, Clark was able to hold on to himself and give a validating response back to her. Marion Solomon and Stan Tatkin (2011), coming from both a psychobiological and an attachment perspective, offered many suggestions about how to help couples handle their arousal with each other and recapture safety in their relationship, although they do this work in a manner Narrative Therapists would find quite directive. Mona Fishbane (2013) also presented her way of working with couples, influenced by many of the same neurobiological ideas found in this book.

In Clark and Karen's dialogue, we then got a glimpse of a memory that contained the kind of stored implicit affect that was contributing to Karen's "steel barrier" response. These feelings created the visceral experience she was speaking about and continued to influence the conclusions she came to about herself. My attempt to juxtapose the old memory and conclusions with more recent developments and to invited conclusions about herself in this context reflect the influence of literature on memory reconsolidation (Ecker, Ticic, & Hulley, 2012; Ecker 2015a, 2015b, 2015c). My understanding about memory is that it is also state dependent, so I was hoping that the pain Karen felt and the pain Clark felt in response would open Clark up to his own pain. Indeed, Clark brought forth his pain about his dad for the first time before switching out of it. Once clients begin allowing themselves to feel the affect contained in certain memories, the affect can be slowly scaffolded into their awareness. These issues are also discussed in Chapter 6.

If technology is influencing our minds to change our brains in ways that have good effects for adaptation to our current cultural context but some bad effects on selves and relationships, then how important is it that we do all we can to work with our minds to change our brains to get the effects that we want? Being more tuned into ourselves (see Chapter 4) and more tuned into others is a start. Nevertheless, once you become focused on the right brain, you open the door to scary stuff.

Ready to go to what might feel like the really "dark side" for Narrative Therapists?

Chapter 6

Nonconscious Influences in Narrative Therapy

Stuff that's hidden and murky and ambiguous is
scary because you don't know what it does.
—Jerry Garcia

I'm hoping you will do an exercise with me, designed to give you an experience that will help you more personally enter into some of the concepts in this chapter that are difficult and strange to Narrative Therapists.

First, to prepare, read through the questions below. Now, imagine a recent time when you had a somewhat stressful interpersonal experience with a significant other. Next, breathe and picture this MOMENT. Take a few minutes to go through as much of the detail of this experience that you need to help reexperience it—if you are not feeling it as you are picturing it, you are not reexperiencing it! As you are reexperiencing it, try to notice the following:

• Are you losing hold of your preferred self, and is another version taking over?

- Is there a surge of energy in your body? Or a general dampening and desire to leave? Or both?
- Are particular memories popping out?
- Does the experience seem just annoying, or is it feeling bigger, more "dangerous"?
- Is the experience affecting your sense of safety and security?

Now I am curious about the aftereffects of this stressful experience on you and your relationships. You could reflect and respond, or go back into the MOMENT to get closer to the experience:

- Did you share what happened with someone else, and was this comforting?
- Did you find yourself "discharging" the stress on others around you, being more quick to erupt? Or maybe you were just more clingy?
- Did you find yourself more distant and disconnected from yourself and others?
- Did you have any experience of something(s) from the past being activated, a vague sense that more was involved than just what occurred, an unsettledness that hung around?

I'm going to access my internalized version of the main clients you have met in the preceding chapters and imagine their response to this exercise:

Matt: As my girlfriend is telling me that she is going out with friends, I'm quickly losing hold of my calm, responsive, friendly self, and a want-to-hurt-her self is taking over. I'm feeling a surge of anger, and I'm yelling. I'm totally aroused. I'm remembering all the times she has done this before. I flashed on my last girlfriend telling me she wanted to spend the night at her place. I'm really desperate . . . I get this way with girlfriends. I'm ruminating about being alone. I only told you about this, Jeff, and it helped, a little. I drank some. I refused to see her for a couple of days afterward. I wish I knew what was going on with me.

Doug: I'm getting mad at someone who I'm feeling is not doing a job well. I'm generally distant, suspicious, and critical of others, so this is not unusual. I have a mellow version that only used to come out when I attended Grateful Dead shows. I don't remember much about the past . . . I couldn't tell you what was going on in my body or how I felt. I'm thinking about the other times I failed like this. I don't generally feel safe. I never share with anyone, I medicate . . . I'm always unsettled.

Karen: In the MOMENT I am feeling discounted, and I disconnect quickly after a brief flurry. I'm in my self-protective version, and I stay that way until something pulls me back. This is very unsafe. Afterward, I would not let the person near me. I thought only about the times he hurt me and how little I am valued. This experience felt very familiar to me, and very big.

Clark: I'm feeling shut out, and the generally mellow and easygoing me has become pushy and demanding. I hate this . . . Why can't we stay close? I'm reacting quickly and can't seem to let go. Karen always does this . . . Later, I became clingy, wanting reassurance. It seemed big. I'm like this for quite a while. I'm thinking about this all the time, and I'm depressed.

Identities

In Narrative Therapy we are interested in separating individuals from Problem identities and helping them enter into more preferred versions, ones that bring good effects into their lives. With many if not most clients, finding experiences in their lives that fall out of their dominant Problem story is not challenging if you take a wide account of the effects of the Problem. Usually what become noticeable are some areas or times when the Problem has less influence. There are situations, however, when finding and/or bringing forth possibilities is much more difficult: when the Problem has been around a long time, or when a long time ago developmental trauma set a Problem-influenced direction in motion. What makes these Problem identities so recalcitrant, so difficult to leave behind? What makes alternative ones so difficult to step into and hold?

I have already noted that Narrative Therapy rejects the notion of a single, true self and instead embraces the idea of multiple identities or multiple versions of the self; Interpersonal Neurobiology agrees. Dan Siegel stated: "From an interpersonal neurobiology perspective, the view of a 'unified self' is missing the point of the multiplicity of our normal, adaptive, ever-changing healthy selves" (2012b, p. 35). He went on to suggest that we need these multiple selves to handle the diverse demands of our lives. Neurobiologically, a *self* is a brain state, a state of mind. Because we all have more than one brain state, more than one state of mind, we have more than one self available to us. States of mind are clusters of neural firing patterns that have emotions, thoughts, certain behaviors, moods, and access to particular memories embedded within them. They are adaptive, because the brain likes to efficiently organize the ability to respond. We all have states that are more or less dominant; those that are dominant and have more influence have more experience behind them. Over time, these states can become increasingly complex and organized into larger patterns. They can be activated at any given moment or can be more enduring. A state that is frequently engaged might be labeled a "personality" or a trait. For example, when circuits of anger, fear, or sadness/loss are heavily used, these neural pathways become stronger and more influential. It is easy to see that, when viewed through the lens of the idea of a true self, these appear to be a fixed, permanent "personality." Furthermore, because our brain likes coherence, it has a bias for making the world appear solid and stable. To do so, it constructs an unbroken picture, giving us a continuous sense of a self out of these multiple brain states.

Not surprising to those of us who did Family Systems work back in the day, however, is that these states are context dependent. They also may have us acting/reacting in certain ways, without experiencing any purposeful intentions to do so. In effect, the context represents a set of cues or triggers that the brain recognizes as one where a particular state is relevant and useful. That it is useful might be old news, because the current context might not be one where the particular state is helpful, despite its familiarity to the brain. Narrative Therapy tries to reduce the influence of these Problem states by making the effects of the state noticeable (externalization) and by integrating other, more preferred responses into an alternative state, in effect thickening the neural network that supports these currently nondominant states.

As implied in Chapter 5, one way to think about being with others is as an interacting process of mutual multiple identities (states of mind). Again, given the influence of Family Systems approaches, it is not a new idea to us that our responses to others have the effect of inviting particular responses, which depend on the emotional meaning for the other person, and that this process can become patterned; we saw this with Clark and Karen's Push–Pull Back cycle. Now we understand that these responses are influenced by certain states of mind that are evoked by the relational context. Shifting from one state of mind to another happens fluidly and is reactive to the situational triggers; we don't necessarily experience that a different identity has emerged, or that the new one is being invited out by the others around us.

Raymundo, a forty-two-year-old Latino, heterosexual computer programmer, arrived at our session with a frown plastered on his face. My hopes of being able to thicken the small strand of New Story we constructed in the last session were immediately dashed, because I had learned that when Raymundo was in this "place," attempting to do anything but focus on his negative experiences had negative effects, as I described briefly in Chapter 4.

Raymundo lives in one side of a town house; his estranged wife occupies the other side. His middle-school-age daughter floats between the two dwellings—a metaphor that a former Systems Therapist but long turned Narrative Therapist couldn't completely dismiss. A therapist (who had been working with the daughter for bulimia, and was now working with the couple) referred Raymundo to me; feeling that his angry responses to his wife and daughter needed individual attention. Raymundo was born in Chile, where he lived until moving to the United States in grade school. His father died when Raymundo was in high school. His mom has carried a diagnosis of paranoid schizophrenia since her suicide attempt when Raymundo was six. According to Raymundo, she loves him but is intrusive and frustrating and rarely responds directly to him about anything. She does "weird things," and he is worried that he is weird like her. His wife, a CPA, suffers from chronic fatigue syndrome. He had seen his previous therapist for many years.

As was often the case over the many times we had been meeting, Ray-

mundo began by complaining about his poor standing with his boss at work and consequent fears of being laid off, his rejection by his wife, his daughter's eating problems, his inability to go over bridges or ride elevators to high floors, and, in general, his relationship with himself ("I'm weird," "I'm not smart enough"). The darkness spread quickly over the room like the fog that comes into San Francisco during a summer late afternoon.

R: I've had so many critical feelings lately . . .

J: Can you tell me when these Critical Feelings have been around during the last couple of weeks?

R: At work (he describes them) . . .

J: Where else have these Critical Feelings been giving you a hard time?

R: With myself, with my kid, with my wife.

J: What do the Critical Feelings have to say about all this?

R: I'm a loser; I don't go anywhere or do anything outside of work . . .

J: What's it like for you, for these Critical Feelings to be taking your life away?

R: I feel helpless, powerless, trapped. It makes me feel like such a failure.

J: That must be horrible for you. Where in your . . .

R: (interrupting) Sorry, no wait . . . I'm worried I will be laid off at work. My boss doesn't know what he is doing. He's weird . . .

We have had conversations like this many times. It's often a fight to hold on to my therapist self and not simply continue this same conversation over and over again. I have to work hard to not let all the unspoken affect in the room scare me off or deaden me and shut me down. How do we understand all that is going on here?

Memory

To go further into the discussion of identities, we need to know something about memory. Siegel (2012b) suggested that memory is the way the past influences a process in the future—a neural pathway with more influence. He described it as a change in the probability of activating a neural network pattern in the future. The more experience behind it, the greater the probability the memory will be activated and influential. Narrative Therapy has always implicitly accepted what neurobiology acknowledges: all experience is encoded. How strongly it is encoded is the issue. Our concept of Unique Outcome MOMENTS (UOMs) is based on the assumption that clients potentially have access to these unstoried experiences.

What facilitates memory is emotional arousal, novelty, repetition, and focused attention. Emotions are important because they activate memories of times when we felt similarly. For example, in my last conversation with Karen and Clark (see Chapter 5), feeling Karen's pain evoked Clark's pain. Emotional arousal also influences the encoding of experience. So, what happens when we solicit a memory, when we Re-member (the Narrative idea of bringing forth particular relationship experiences that support a more preferred story)? We construct a new neural network profile from the old, as memories from other experiences we have had subsequent to the original memory, as well as our current state, influence the old one. In other words, once a memory is brought forward, it goes back in a way that's altered; it might be stronger, weaker, or simply different. Siegel quoted his "memory mentor" Robert Bjork: "Memory retrieval is a memory modifier" (2010a, p. 200).

To use a familiar Narrative question, who would be least surprised to know that how, when, and where we invite these memories are so critical? From Michael White and David Epston: "The questions we ask about events and the realities we construct . . . determine the very distinctions that we 'pull out' from the world" (1990, p. 5). When we ask questions, we are quite literally creating a new reality in newly formed neural networks. These new networks will be "thin" at first; more questions and other narrative practices (e.g., letters, teams) are needed to thicken them, to give them more experience so that they have more influence.

What are the different types of memory? What's in our heads in the moment is called *working memory*, which contains what we need to make decisions in the moment. On the other hand, what might be influencing us are *implicit memories*, aspects of experience we encode without attention and awareness; these might be behaviors, emotional reactions, perceptions, or bodily sensations. Implicit memories are emotional memories stored in the amygdala and begin to form at birth. If they get "stuck" in the amygdala, one effect they have is to generate impulsive reactions, because they become influential without involving any cognitive reflection. It is useful to think of implicit memories not as unconscious but as *nonconscious*, operating without conscious awareness. These memories become mental models, stored experiences in visceral form, which influence our narratives. Mental processes (e.g., mood, motivation) can be implicit, too. We may be aware of the effects of these but don't really get that our response is being influenced by previous experiences stored in our brain, that our state of mind is implicitly shaping our perceptions, intentions, and reasoning.

In the years before his death, White (2004, 2005) became interested in the effects of implicit memories, particularly in the area of trauma. In a collection of his writings published posthumously, White discussed a piece of supervision he was doing with Judy, who reported meeting with a family and experiencing "a 'negative psychological reaction' that she found quite painful." White "asked her to describe the sort of images of life and identity that might be triggered" and invited "her to speculate about what it was in the history of her own lived experience that might be resonating." Judy's meeting with this family had brought up "painful memories of rejection that she'd felt from her own parents" and a "longing" that "she was not generally conscious of" (2011, pp. 73–78).

Raymundo was telling me that his estranged wife didn't invite him to a gathering of her family, which made sense to me but was hurtful to him:

J: What effect did it have on you when your wife didn't invite you?
R: Shame and embarrassment.
J: Have you had this kind of experience before?
R: You mean recently?
J: I mean when you were younger.
R: I'm not sure.
J: Can you imagine the MOMENT when you realized you were uninvited?
R: OK . . . I'm trying . . . Not sure . . .
J: How about I help you—where were you . . .

R: You're only making it harder . . . when you talk I lose my thoughts.

J: OK, I'll shut up.

R: It happened yesterday. I was upset . . . I'm remembering . . .

J: Where do you feel the upset in your body?

R: You know I don't like it when you ask that question . . . (feeling his body) In my chest.

J: Do you remember having that feeling in your chest before?

R: When I was in high school.

J: (surprised that he stayed with it) Could you tell me about it?

R: I was dancing with a girl during a formal, and I became angry and upset.

J: What effects did this have then?

R: I wondered what was wrong with me.

J: What effects are these feelings having now?

R: I'm still weird . . . at times I think you're weird, too.

J: Thanks for letting me know that . . . I get it. Are you feeling that way now?

This was actually progress. As usual, he reacted to my questions as if I was being intrusive (I guess we therapists are), but eventually he was willing to enter questions that threatened to bring up uncomfortable feelings. I was always imagining that his body was full of these scary feelings, many of which were unstoried and had been around a very long time. Even after many sessions, it was still frightening to him to let me in; Lack of Safety and Distrust influenced all of his relationships.

As a child begins to grow, a narrator emerges. By the age of two we can tell and understand stories; we can look into the past, present, and future. *Explicit memories* begin to develop at about a year and a half and continue to develop until about the age of five. There are two kinds of explicit memories: factual (left hemisphere) and episodic or autobiographical (right hemisphere). We use these explicit memories to assemble pieces (including implicit memories) into whole stories; explicit memory is required to fully story our lives. These "landscapes of action" serve as internal search engines to explore lived experience. Explicit memories are stored in the hippocampus and involve fine distinctions between events past and present. Joseph LeDoux (1996) made a very important distinction between the memories of emotions stored in the hippocampus and actual emotional memories stored in the amygdala. It is the emotional memories in the amygdala that need to be retrieved for substantive change to take place. In the usual developmental course, the higher limbic areas and cortex take over for the amygdala, resulting in less reactivity and more mature decision making over time (Montgomery, 2013).

In the hippocampus, explicit and implicit memories are integrated, providing a sense of context. Siegel (2010b, 2012a) suggested that with chronic ongoing stress or trauma, this integrative function can be damaged, affecting one's ability to put events in context. He pointed to various pieces of research that have found a reduction in the size of hippocampi in soldiers returning from war and in those who have experienced childhood sexual abuse. There is, however, some debate about cause and effect. Has previous stress (even stress passed down through the sperm and egg from previous generations) caused something referred to as limbic kindling, a sensitivity to arousal and hyperemotionality, creating more vulnerability to future traumatic experiences?

Trauma involves divided attention, and attention is required for the hippocampus to be activated. The hormones activated during stressful events impede hippocampal functioning but unfortunately increase the implicit encoding of fear. Siegel described the adaptive process where, during traumatic events, our minds dampen the neural passage of energy and information from subcortical levels to the prefrontal cortex, diverting our attention from what is happening and reducing pain and concomitant toxic chemical overload in the brain. The effect is less explicit storying, but with more implicit memories floating around in the body without the context of a story to contain them. These implicit memories continue to shape our subjective feelings without us being able to make sense of them. Lacking a story and thus a sense of context, they are not tagged as the past. Siegel (2010a) believes that we end up with two streams of awareness: a narrative stream, where concepts are in story form, and one of raw emotion, as if it is happening now: the implicit reactivation of memory. These memories become part of our top-down influences, but in a way that is not integrated with either the factual or autobiographical aspects of explicit memory. Implicit reactivation can shut down our ability to notice either our own responses in the moment or the context in which they are occurring.

Our minds can thus use the brain to block something from access in order to protect ourselves and our brain from pain. This is an adaptation that can occur around any material that is painful, not just severe trauma. In effect, our minds construct a version that does not include information from our internal emotional states. Maybe you can imagine the experiences that someone like Doug went through that helped him arrive at just such an adaptation, one where he was not feeling what was in his body. Over time, external stimulation from relationships and the environment become less and less integrated with body-based internal reactions such as feelings.

How can we deal with the effects of implicit memories so that we can begin to build story and context around them? Eye Movement Desensitization and Reprocessing (EMDR) is one popular technique to loosen the influence of these implicit memories (Shapiro, 2013), which can be used in conjunction with Narrative Therapy. The theory behind this technique focuses on the importance of the Adaptive Information Processing of experience. All perceptions of events are stored as memories in neural networks and become the basis for interpreting ongoing experience. These physiologically stored memory networks contain disturbing memories (they can be trauma related or just life events) stored just as they were experienced (this includes childlike emotions if the experiences occurred during childhood). These memories are stored in isolation and contain the affects, thoughts, physical sensations, behavioral responses, and most important, arousal responses involved in the experience. The influence of these previously experienced life events can be triggered by circumstance or context. Francine Shapiro (2013) suggested that because of the high levels of distress involved in these experiences, they are unable to be linked to anything adaptive, such as later-formed contradictory experiences. Because memory is stored associatively, the etiological event that generated the distress is not always apparent. If EMDR is effective, connections are made that guide the client adaptively, and the negative emotions are no longer present when the client thinks of the event. Interestingly, eye movements are a basic SEEKING system response, suggesting that this primary emotional system is activated in this approach.

It has been my experience for some time now that bringing forth Problem/autobiographical MOMENTS can capture the influence of these unprocessed memories and that when a client enters into these emotions new meanings often spontaneously occur. Along these lines, I was very excited to discover Memory Reconsolidation Therapy (MRT). Bruce Ecker's theory (Ecker, Ticic, & Hulley, 2012; Ecker, 2015a, 2015b, 2015c) is that when psychotherapy is successful, memory reconsolidation has taken place. According to Ecker, any learning that occurs in the presence of strong emotion becomes locked into subcortical implicit memory circuits by special synapses; until the late 1990s this locking was considered permanent. Similar to the thinking behind Adaptive Information Processing, this implicit learning is considered an encapsulated state that keeps memories insulated from and thus immune to learning from new knowledge or experience. The effect of these memories being kept locked away and separate is that, despite them being retriggered regularly (e.g., Matt being unlovable or Karen being "Small") and receiving strong disconfirming responses from others, the old conclusions don't change.

Subsequent research has revealed that these memories can indeed be brought forth and unlocked (i.e., deconsolidated). Once this happens, new learning must occur concomitantly to change the self stories, or identity conclusions, that had been influenced by the original learning. Because these memories will then exist in explicit memory, they will still be remembered, but because they are no longer in the implicit memory system, they lose their ability to reactively influence responses and identity conclusions. The work of MRT involves explicitly bringing into awareness both the (emotional) learning experience and then the specific elements of learning associated with it (i.e., the identity conclusions or meaning given to it). Seymour Epstein suggested that "making an implicit experiential belief explicit is an important first step in correcting an experiential belief, because once it is identified in the rational system, it can be treated experientially" (quoted in Armstrong, 2015, p. 80).

In 2004 it was found that, once the original memory is brought forth in the room (with all of the emotion it contains), it is important to evoke counterexperiences that involve conclusions that mismatch those predicted by the original experience (Pedreira et al., as cited in Ecker, 2015b). This finding led to a three-step transformational process:

1. *Activate the memory.* If, in a discussion about the "Problem," it becomes apparent that an emotional memory is influencing it, the memory is evoked (i.e., a past Problem MOMENT), and then the conclusions that were arrived at based on the experience are brought forth. These conclusions may have already been discussed or may be obvious but it is new to reexperience the emotional learning first and then face these conclusions. In effect, you are bringing forth the constructed mental model used by the brain to make predictions about the world for survival reasons.

2. *Unlock the memory with a mismatch.* Once mismatched with an alternative experience—a UOM in Narrative terms—the memory is unlocked. This creates a labile state in which the memory is available to be influenced by new learning for about five hours, after which reconsolidation occurs.

3. *Revise with new learning.* Ecker suggested that, for revision to occur, the new learning must involve visceral emotional experience and not be just conceptual (again, a MOMENT in my terminology). Revisions can also involve pairing something like EMDR or tapping (instead of the more traditionally transacted verbal experience) with the original memory. Juxtaposition between old and new appears to be the key to unlocking the special synapses (Ecker, 2015b), with three repetitions of the juxtaposed experience engaged in with clients, going back and forth from the past emotional memory and its related conclusions to the new learning, to accomplish this.

Ecker (2015a, 2015b) noted important distinctions between this process and the process of the behavioral idea of extinction. In extinction, nothing is unlearned, because separate learning occurs in a separate memory system, which competes with the (unchanged) original learning. The new learning occurs in the prefrontal areas, not in the amygdala, where emotional memory resides, with the effect that the new learning is influential except when the old learning is retriggered. In contrast, with MRT, the old learning permanently loses its influence. Perhaps some of our Restorying efforts would fall into the former category, as often clients enact the New Story unless the context invites out the old one.

As I have discussed, most models have questions or practices that juxtapose the Problem with an alternative (e.g., bifurcation questions discussed in Chapter 3). Clearly these ideas can be incorporated into any therapy model; Ecker believes that this process accounts for change in all models: "EMDR, tapping, and progressive counting utilize a dual focus procedure in which conscious awareness is anchored to a sensory stimulus in the safe present environment while also attending internally to the traumatic emotional learning underlying the symptom" (2015b, p. 77).

In a traditional Narrative Therapy interview, where externalizations are paired with Unique Outcomes and in effect juxtaposed, perhaps the memory reconsolidation process is occasionally initiated. What might be the effect of going about our usual process with some of these MRT principles in mind? Problem-supporting emotional memories can be brought forth, and then clients' conclusions about their identity or about relationships, and then effects and positions on these effects. The UOM can then be juxtaposed with the Problem memories, going back and forth several times between them. But, once again, care must be taken to have externalizations ultimately reflect past emotional learning and not just current experience, before the conclusions involved in these old but influential experiences are brought forth. Of course, the alternative experiences must be in the form of MOMENTS to assure they feel experientially real to the client.

In Chapter 5 I showed the influence of these ideas on my work with Karen. I hope you are beginning to picture the real effects of these memories and to have some ideas about how to address these effects. Here is an experience I had with Raymundo that illustrates one of these effects:

J: Hey, Raymundo . . . you can go on back to my office (I stop to get something out of an open closet I pass on the way to my office) . . .

R: (Goes into the room)

J: How's it going?

R: I've been in a bad mood.

J: (warmly) What effects has this bad mood had?

R: I'm not happy . . . (angrily) my doctors don't help me, my boss doesn't help me, and you haven't helped me. I've been coming here a long time, and I still have the same Problems . . .

J: How horrible it is for you to be plagued by these bad moods. Let's talk some more about your feelings about our work.

I suspect I am not alone in having the experience of a client (or colleague, friend, or family member) unload (or upload) their feelings. In Raymundo's case, this response can be triggered by just about anything that feels like abandonment to him and comes with the concomitant conclusion of his own lack of worth to others. The neurobiology behind this kind of response, and how our lived experiences shape these responses, will hopefully be enlightening. Afterward, I return to the topic of identities.

We Are Hardwired to Handle Stressful Situations in Specific Ways

The autonomic nervous system (ANS), which mediates our response to threat, is made up of two branches: the sympathetic nervous system (SNS) and parasympathetic nervous system (PSNS). These are systems of involuntary responses that contain pathways to glands, blood vessels, and organs and affect digestion, heart rate, breathing, and sexual arousal. The SNS branch, which is excitatory, moderates our flight-or-fight response in situations appraised as dangerous. It does so by increasing stress hormone output, heart rate, and blood pressure while decreasing the need for food, sex, and elimination. The effect of increased arousal is a tight engagement with the external environment and a high level of energy mobilization and utilization. The PSNS branch, which is inhibitory, moderates rest and repair, growth hormones, eating, sex, and elimination. It decreases or dampens arousal, resulting in disengagement from the external environment, freezing, and utilization of low levels of energy in situations appraised as involving a threat to one's life.

The ANS also mediates our response to *internal* threats (i.e., to situations that involve our affective responses), as it is connected to the subcortical areas that generate arousal and autonomic bodily based aspects of emotions. Like with most systems mediated by the brain, ANS responses are shaped by genetic predisposition, ordinary and extraordinary life experiences, and the circumstances at hand.

Stephen Porges (2009, 2011) has suggested what he calls the Polyvagal Theory to account for a multilevel response to stress. He posited a hierarchy of response, where the newer system overrides the older ones. It is called *polyvagal* because the theory suggests that mammals, especially primates, seem to have evolved a second branch of the vagal nerve, allowing for the development of a social engagement system (SES). The vagal nerve extends from the brainstem to the stomach and has connections to several organs, including the heart and lungs. According to Porges, our initial response to stress is influenced by the newer, myelinated (fast) ventral vagus, which allows for rapid engagement and disengagement by lowering cardiac output, which reduces SNS responding. This leads to a calmer response to handle pain and unpleasantness. This calm state allows for the use of the SES, which helps dispense with SNS hypervigilance and instead facilitates proximity and contact. Using the newer system allows for a minimization of the biological costs and concomitant health risks associated with overreliance on SNS excitement to respond to stressful situations (the SNS is slower to engage and slower to dampen).

The next response in the hierarchy involves an SNS-type response, and the last is a PSNS-type response, mediated by the older, unmyelinated dorsal vagus branch. Using the PSNS prevents cell death caused by SNS hyperarousal by creating severe hypoarousal and pain blunting. Overuse of the PSNS, however, can lead to a complete shutdown, ranging from extremely low breathing (not so good especially for mammals) to fainting. For those with chronic, severe SNS use, hyperarousal is often followed by hypoarousal. Over time, this SNS-PSNS cycle leads to a loss of ventral function and a dominance of the dorsal branch. The clinical implications of these ANS issues will soon become clear.

Because this newer vagal branch subdues limbic reactivity, enables higher cortical control, and manages visceral responses, it allows social behavior to be the first step in seeking safety. Porges also suggested that this newer social branch enables caretaking and compassion. The caring listener emits little sighs, lowering the fight-or-flight response (SNS) for the speaker and the listener. Shari Geller and Stephen Porges (2014) believe that safety is communicated by these physiological markers of social engagement, which are mediated by the vagus nerve (a right-brain to right-brain communication). For example, social engagement is facilitated by regulating facial muscles to cue safety and danger. Geller and Porges conclude that the all important relationship factors in psychotherapy are transacted in this manner.

However, to whatever extent someone has learned that interpersonal connection is not safe, there is a concomitant inability to use the SES and inhibit SNS and PSNS responses in what could be a safe environment (called false positives, when something is responded to as dangerous when it is not). Effects of this unhelpful experiential learning include physical Problems (e.g., elevated heart rate and blood pressure due to overuse of the SNS) and Problems that take over to manage the escalating arousal (e.g., acting out, overcontrol). Furthermore, an experience of danger (correctly assessed or not) comes with a biological response (heart rate, etc.) that in turn influences the story that is being created and the responses that are then encouraged.

One more comment on this vagal system: a transitory depression of the SES sometimes occurs while we are evaluating intentionality. Because we are hardwired to make conclusions about intentionality through our mirror neuron system and to react to others depending on the conclusions we reach, we are initially cautious in responding to others until their intentions are made clear. Again, based on our previous experiences, this may lead to too much or not enough caution in any particular relational situation. I am sure that everyone has noticed, whether in clinical or in personal situations, that social isolation is an effect of Problems, although sometimes overly clingy behavior might be a substitute:

Matt: I have no tolerance for any possible disengagement by my significant other, stressed or not.

Doug: I don't really get engagement.

Clark: When I feel stressed, I desperately want my significant others to be involved with me and want it immediately. I guess, without realizing it, at other times I get pushy when I feel I'm not being involved.

Karen: It doesn't take much for me to disengage. If I sense even a little diminishment by someone, I don't really think about what's happening, I just quickly shut down . . . it's too frightening.

Raymundo: I want to be cared for but nobody would care for me. I'm too weird, and people can be hard to deal with.

As I have been suggesting, some of what determines our response to stress is our previous experience in similar situations. We all have a window of tolerance, an amount of stress we can tolerate and still hold on to our preferred selves. According to Siegel (2010a, 2010b), the width of the window is specific to the state of mind we are in at that moment. For example, the particular state of mind that reflects our ability to tolerate fear depends on our internal context (our own experiences and wiring), as well as the external context at hand. Within the window, Siegel suggested, one's span of arousal maintains a flow, where middle prefrontal cortex functions are engaged and one can maintain response flexibility. Using a river metaphor to describe this flow, Siegel suggested that when we can't maintain ourselves within this window, we crash into one bank or the other. On one side, we reduce our functioning into too narrow a space and get rigid; we appear flat, incongruent, often nonverbal. On the other side, we are too expansive and chaotic; we become very reactive. One really important implication of all of this is that Problems are about the *amount* of arousal one is experiencing—Problems reflect the intensity of the affect, not whether the affect is positive or negative.

Under low stress (this describes most normal life stressors) and in situations that involve control of well-established patterns of behavior under ordinary and familiar circumstances, we generally have only midrange arousal and experience familiar levels of anxiety, apprehension, worry, rumination, and muscle tension. In these instances, our left brain inhibits right-brain emotional expression. As stated earlier, our left brain is less emotional and more motor dominant and involves voluntary, conscious thought and verbal communication. With our left brains taking over, the cognitions and the overt behavior we need to address the situation are maintained. Allen Schore (2012) suggested that cognitive and insight-oriented therapies are best suited to these Problems. Interestingly, Schore cites a Cognitive Behavioral Therapy study by Siegel et al., which suggested that it is more effective with lower levels of depression (less stress). Apparently, using Cognitive Behavioral Therapy techniques to manage higher levels of stress and affect results in self-control degrading over time, with overuse affecting one's ability to monitor and control oneself in other spheres. The suggestion here is that using a left-brain strategy to handle a right-brain problem is a losing battle, given the strong influence of affect and the limited capacity of working memory to maintain a cognitive approach.

A previous article (Zimmerman & Beaudoin, 2015) suggested that assisting clients in bringing forth affective material that sits at the edge of their window of tolerance would be a useful scaffolding approach. Indeed, Narrative Therapy has long advocated bringing forth Unique Outcomes by imagining how far the influence of a Problem might extend and then noting the limits of its influence on the client, in effect at the border of the window of tolerance. As an example, for Raymundo interpersonal relationships outside of the work context brings with them more affect than he can bear, but at work it is manageable some of the time. A question to him might be, "I see that Lack of Safety has gotten in your way of getting together with people outside of work. How have you been able to stop it from silencing you with coworkers?" I could then ask him about his skills and knowledge in the work situation. At any rate, Raymundo has only so much tolerance for intimacy, and you can see where his window begins and ends.

Narrative Therapists have been asking Unique Outcome questions like this to good effect for a long time. I now realize that doing so without attention to emotion is more effective when you are dealing with a left-brain Problem, a stress. However, when the Problem is bigger, when we are dealing with the influence of what feels like more threatening affect (e.g., Raymundo), the affect must be brought in more directly to have the biggest effect. UOMs offer one possibility to address those issues; bringing forth the affective experience of the MOMENT allows affective tolerance to be scaffolded.

As implied, when stress increases, or attempts to manage it fail, the right brain begins to take over from the left brain. Schore (2012) suggested that each hemisphere has a unique window of arousal tolerance, leading him to posit a Window of Affective Tolerance. At either end of an inverted U-shape (arousal too high to too low), left-brain functions disorganize and become less efficient, but the right brain becomes more organized, efficient, and dominant. Its different range of arousal tolerance allows the right brain to sustain its nonconscious survival functions under high stress and allows it to manage situations experienced as dangerous (with a high-arousal SNS response), as well as those experienced as a life threat (with a low-arousal PSNS response). Schore suggested that, in any case, each window has its limits, a range in which affect is able to be handled, or regulated. Dysregulated affect is triggered at the upper limits of the window; when this occurs, the cortical-subcortical components get uncoupled (i.e., reason has less influence over reactivity).

Human Connections Shape Neural Connections

What I have been talking around is our ability to regulate our own affect, an area of study that Schore (2009) labeled Affect Regulation Theory. What contributes to each person's unique ability to manage affect in different contexts? To soothe themselves? To manage arousal without Problems taking over? Neurobiologists believe that learning affect regulation begins when an infant signals a need and a caretaker receives that signal and regulates emotion through being attuned and responsive to the child's emotional state. This relational process of attending in this manner structures the infant's developing neural circuitry in a way that enables the infant to increasingly exercise self-regulation as neural pathways become stronger. Not responding to the infant or responding in a manner that does not have a regulating effect will lead to the opposite result: a right hemisphere that does not swiftly transfer information between cortical (thinking) and subcortical (affect) systems. According to Schore, the left brain is never directly involved in regulating, calling again into question left-brain therapeutic approaches for difficult Problems. The overall point here is that an adult attunement to the child's emotions will result in developing the kind of neural structure that supports the ability to have balanced response flexibility.

When the caretaker matches the child's implicit affective-arousal states (a right-brain to right-brain nonconscious process involving, for example, tone and facial expressions), the child experiences the caretaker's state as if it was the child's own, which has the regulating effect. It is easy to imagine that this effect is similar to the one in a therapy process. What becomes balanced is the right-brain-managed ANS. Individuals whose early experiences involve this kind of emotional responsiveness can flexibly make use of both branches of the ANS as the situation warrants, because their window of tolerance will likely be large, and they will have built neural structure that supports more balanced responding. Not having this kind of responsiveness leads to the opposite result; in effect, the caretaker induces stress instead of modulating it.

Individuals who received responses from caretakers that were dysregulating rather than responsive or soothing might experience more regular and more easily triggered SNS arousal, particularly when they perceive the emotional responses in the interpersonal environment to be low in affect. Given their high arousal levels, they amp things up by erupting verbally and engaging in more pronounced fight-or-flight responses. Examples of Problems that emerge to manage this arousal are acting out and verbal or physical bullying (Montgomery, 2013). Over time it becomes increasingly difficult to dampen the SNS and enable the SES. If this direction continues, more and more extreme responses evolve, and the harmful amount of stress hormones (e.g., cortisol) generated can become toxic to the brain and body. At that point, the PSNS kicks in to protect the brain from toxic chemical overload by suppressing the SNS. On the interpersonal front, hyperarousal (SNS responding) tends to be particularly destructive to relationships (Swan & Scott, 2009).

In contrast, individuals whose experience leads them more easily to PSNS dampening are quick to find discomfort with what they perceive to be too much emotion. This difficulty leads to Problems that damp things down, for example, Overcontrolling, Intellectualization, Obsessiveness, Perfectionism, and, in extreme cases, Dissociation (Montgomery, 2013). Avoidance captures these individuals, as emotional currents seem too strong, and downloading them into their consciousness seems too painful.

And those whose caretakers, instead of modulating stress, induce it without repair (e.g., through abuse or trauma) end up with the kind of two-stage response suggested earlier: first hyperarousal (SNS), a fear state characterized by hypervigilance, and then Dissociation (PSNS), when emotional pain is blocked from consciousness and detachment occurs from the environment and from oneself. In this case, the insula manages a detached connection between emotional evaluation and physiological response. When this process becomes someone's primary regulatory strategy, it comes with a metabolic shutdown, where bodily functioning becomes slow and energy needs to be conserved.

Both SNS- and PSNS-dominated individuals show highs and lows that are too extreme, too prolonged, and too rapidly cycled. They react more strongly to small stressors, even the stress of a therapeutic misattunement. For those whose responses are SNS generated, these are low-threshold, high-intensity reactions followed by a slow return to baseline or Dissociation. When a Problem takes this form, it has the person under its influence experiencing a sharp increase in arousal, resulting in a tremendous pressure to off-load (or upload, as I call it with my Silicon Valley clients), which in turn leads them to invite those around them to take on their arousal. Reactivity in this form is often followed by Dissociation; such people are oblivious to their reactions and the effects they have on others. Sorry, Narrative folks, but in the defense mechanism literature this SNS process is labeled Projective Identification, not a term I ever thought I would use. This term is only a description, from a particular theoretical perspective, that tries to address an SNS-arousal-based response.

The therapeutic context is not immune from interactions like these; clients may attempt, through repeated attributions and considerable acting out in the form of verbal pressuring, to try to upload their painful implicit affect on the clinician. For us therapists, we first experience this invitation in our bodies, with our right brain tipping us off that we have picked something up from our client. Philip Bromberg (2011) suggested that these effects can include excitement, rage, elation, terror, disgust, shame, and the hopeless despair that we have taken on from the client. If we are not resonating, if the invitation to upload is turned down, the effects on us may include boredom, irritation, hostility, and an experience of not really understanding our client. In either case, our being triggered may be reflected at "ordinary" levels; we make a gesture, change posture, modify our tone (tone of voice is hardwired in our brains for adaptive value and is nonconsciously experienced by our client). I have found it helpful to become aware of my own verbal and nonverbal behavioral responses that indicate I am experiencing something uncomfortable to me nonconsciously. Bromberg believes that MOMENTS such as these, however, become an opportunity to help our clients regulate their affect but require our ability to bear the affect.

Here is an e-mail trail between me and a client that demonstrates this desire to upload:

J: Unfortunately, the only other times I have available to do the school visit are 12/10 at 10:45 . . . or during your appointment on 11/20, 12/3, or 12/10 at 2:30.

N: Please try to switch some of your appointments. This visit is very important.

J: I have nowhere to switch them to. Some clients need certain times. I might be able to switch my 12/10 at 9:30 to 10:30 and if so you could have 9:45. Should I find out?

N: Please either switch or try to cancel another appointment. Please try your best. I have tried to be very flexible to meet your tight schedule since we started. Please see if you can come on a day other than days you are in the office, or cancel something. PLEASE . . .

J: I am sorry that I am not able to be as available to you as it seems you feel I should be. I understand that this is important to you; unfortunately, whether in SF or Cupertino, I have extensive commitments to other clients, colleagues, projects, and family members that are equally important to them.

I suspect my tone came through in this e-mail. I watched my client respond this way to school personnel with whom we were working to try to get a better intervention for her daughter, but this time was the first "uploading" on me. When things go badly like this, I might make up a story about my client that puts them in a bad light. Later, when I realize what happened, I make up a story that involves my own deficits as a clinician or a person. Eventually, I store away the visceral cues I experienced and note the storying I engaged in for future reference, to use as cues that I am reacting to the Problem influencing my client in unhelpful ways. I then think about a response I would have preferred to make: "I get that this is really important to you. I can feel your anger and desperation. Is that what it's like for you?" At any rate, not being put off and staying in the relationship are critical (she thanked me so much when her daughter got a good placement).

For those whose responses are PSNS generated, what can happen in the room (if not beforehand) is Dissociation, referred to by Schore as the "ultimate defense" (2011 p. xxiv). As suggested earlier, this involves a mind-body disconnection, where "affect in the body is severed from its corresponding images in the mind, and thereby an unbearably painful meaning is obliterated" (Donald Kalsched, as quoted in Schore, 2011, p. xxiv). Bodily based pain-numbing opiates are elevated as a response to sudden affective hyperarousal, and attention is disengaged from both inner and outer worlds. Dissociation occurs when an area of implicit affect that is not just unpleasant but mentally unbearable is touched; it is then rendered unavailable to cognition. When Dissociation takes over, an internal seduction occurs, as it provides (without awareness) a Problem "smoke detector," an early warning system that anticipates the potential eruption of painful affect (affect dysregulation), with even low levels of stress (Bromberg, 2011). Dissociation quickly takes over the mind, wiping out feelings before they can occur, greatly narrowing the range of the individual's functioning.

Dissociation has the effect of preventing exposure to potential relational learning experiences in intimate contexts (needed for emotional growth) due to overanticipating relational trauma in these contexts. Other effects include an avoidance of novelty, further reducing the likelihood of learning from new emotional experiences; the processing of only left-verbal, not right-emotional tone of voice; and an inability to recall important personal information of a traumatic nature, creating a protective disconnection. Overall, Schore suggested that Dissociation structures a separation of mental processes (e.g., thoughts, emotions, memory) that are normally integrated, making it difficult to process perceptions of the external environment and to integrate them with internal signals (bodily based, felt experience) on a moment-to-moment basis.

All of this prevents access to affective decision making, which is our primary source of appraising value, leading to an impaired ability to adjust and take action on one's behalf. If one can't register affect and pain, then motivational action is gone. For these clients, Bromberg suggested that therapy becomes a means to free the client not from what was done to her "but from what she had to do to herself and to others in order to live with what was done to her in the past" (2011, p. 120).

As I suggested with SNS-influenced responses, the therapist first notices Dissociation as a perceptual phenomenon, feeling the disconnection in the client's body when triggered, yet the client remains unaware. In my case I start to feel sleepy, because, as Bromberg suggested, the therapy context has been drained of emotional meaning. Margaret Wilkinson wrote that she asks herself the following question if feeling this way: "Why this state of mind with this patient at this MOMENT?" (2010, p. 79). Problem MOMENTS are potentially a way to reenter emotional material, but given the client's lack of access to this material, it might be more useful to go to an in-session MOMENT first, to what is happening right now in the room. As previously suggested, what it's like for you to be with client and what it's like for the client to be with you are helpful questions. For example, during a discussion of the upcoming anniversary of my client's mother's death, I noticed and commented, "You just went quiet on me. What happened?" Bromberg believes that this kind of shift to what's happening in the MOMENT involves the therapist inviting the client to name her immediate experience, allowing for the possibility of relearning in states usually avoided. Once the client is in the state, right-brain autobiographical MOMENTS will be activated or available, given state-dependent learning. When I asked my client the question, she responded, "I get a lot of my fears from my mother."

Here's affect I couldn't bear to download:

J: What effect does it have on you when you see your husband acting up like that?

C: (with a pasted-on smile and matter-of-fact tone) Anger and frustration.

J: (my heart really pounding) I know from previous conversations you had some similar experiences growing up.

C: (matter-of-fact) Yes, I lost my dad at an early age. My stepfather and his drinking were imposed on me.

J: (heart still pounding, fighting not to go there, knowing I should) What effect did that have on you?

C: (pasted smile, deadpan) Nobody looked out for me.

J: (defeated) You must have some feelings about that. We should deal with them next time.

I couldn't bear it on that visit, but I was ready for it the next time she came in. Here's another client's affect I was able to download and hold:

J: How's it going?

A: Continuing to decline . . .

J: So sorry to hear that. What do you mean exactly?

A: I'm miserable, despondent.

J: It seems to me that there is like a black blob hanging over you.

A: Now I'm even avoiding some of my professional responsibilities.

J: So the blob is even taking away the last area you were feeling OK about.

A: (tearing up) It's feeling hopeless and unmanageable.

J: It seems so painful . . . I can feel it. Its hard to contain (tearing up).

J: (after some time and more pain acknowledgment) I wish I could help you more.

A: I've always had a resistance . . . probably goes back to Idaho when . . .

This was the first time she acknowledged what seemed obvious to me, that this "resistance" impacted our relationship; perhaps she now felt safe knowing I could bear her emotions. In the next session:

J: How's it going?

A: It hasn't been as soul crushing. I'm beginning to feel like I can handle it.

Here's affect I was able to download after much scaffolding for my client:

N: I felt sick . . . despair (but speaking of this matter-of-factly).

J: When was the last time you experienced feelings like that?

N: I'd just hit someone's car pulling out . . . but this was more like regret and shame.

J: Try picturing it right now. Can you feel those feelings?

N: Not really . . . you know I feel a separation between me and my emotions a lot of the time.

J: Has this been true a long time? Are there times you've been in situations that might have been painful whether you felt it or not?

N: A fourth grade play, my first breakup . . .

J: Let's try picturing that. Can you paint the scene?

N: (He describes it) . . . a line like "It's not working out." It was heart crushing.

I hope you are beginning to appreciate the relationship of biologically based reactions to stress and management of stressful affects contained in implicit memories. Our nervous system is wired to handle external and internal dangers in particular ways, depending on the level of threat. Are you wondering about the adaptive value of implicit memories and the relationship of these memories to identities?

The brain uses experience to make predictions about the world to operate efficiently and to be prepared to handle dangerous situations. Louis Cozolino (2016) made the point that evolution is a bit behind the times, that in today's world too many false positives are created from personal experiences that aren't usefully generalized to the world at large. Problems, as we think about them in Narrative Therapy, emerge from the tension between arousal and affect management and the way people prefer to be with others and live their lives.

Let's check in with Raymundo before thickening the developmental discussion and discussing the relationship between affect, arousal, and identities:

R: I switched groups today. They actually wanted me.

J: How did you get past Anxiety to make the switch happen?

R: I leaned on people, I reached out.

J: Wow! What made . . .

R: (interrupting) It was the response I got.

J: What kind of responses from these people helped you manage the Anxiety?

R: They were kind and responsive.

J: When they responded that way, what did that tell you about how they saw you as a person?

R: That I was competent.

J: What was it like feeling that way?

R: I felt safe.

J: I know safety has been elusive to you. I can just imagine how nice it must be for you to feel safe in that way.

R: There came a point where I couldn't trust mom. I worry about her craziness even now. I couldn't trust her.

J: I'm so sorry you felt that way, that you went through life that way.

R: (looking very upset) I didn't understand what was going on.

J: Oh, Raymundo . . .

R: (abruptly changing the subject) I wanted to talk about my daughter.

J: OK, Raymundo. What's going on with her?

This was the first time Raymundo described being able to enter into his pre-ferred identity of being connected to others. Previously, he would story his disengagement in terms of negative evaluations of both himself and others, but in the end it is usually much too frightening for him to trust others to care about him or for him. It is also hard for him to share these feelings with me. I'm not saying he hasn't experienced connection, but he does so very tentatively and from an experience-distant position. His linking this to what he experienced with his mom was also a first. There was so much emotion in the room; it soon was all he could bear at that point in time, and he changed the subject. I made the choice to follow him and leave these feelings behind, as it seemed like he had gone as far as he could on that visit.

On a Narrative note, Michael White suggested that it might be useful, when working with clients who experienced trauma, to build a platform of safety for them to stand on first, before addressing traumatic material. In the above conversation, for example, drawing out Raymundo's positive relational experience at work may have contributed to his ability to bear the traumatic memories with his mom, even for a bit. In addition, unlike in traditional Narrative work, I am OK with explicitly including my relationship to the client as part of that platform of safety.

Human Connections Shape Neural Connections II

Above I discussed caretakers and infants and the process that occurs between them that helps shape neural structure, particularly between the subcortical areas and the upper right cortex. Schore (2009) discussed studies with the "Still-Face" paradigm, which evaluated effects on infants when caregivers offered no vocalizations and showed no emotionally expressive facial features or gestures. Infants reacted as if they were threatened, showing increased arousal and interactive behaviors, and confusion and fearfulness at the (real) loss of connection. This was followed with such responses as bodily collapse, loss of postural control, withdrawal, gaze aversion, and sadness. Also, for infants, a blank face resulted in greater right-brain activity on a functional magnetic resonance image, similar to someone labeled with posttraumatic stress disorder. Researchers proposed that a dissociation between the emotional evaluation of the event and the physiological reaction to it had been triggered, as the infants eventually detached not only from the environment but also from themselves, their body, their own actions, and their sense of identity. What makes withdrawal of emotional responsiveness from significant others so stressful to infants? Does withdrawal have the same effect on adults as well?

Human babies are born with a head size small enough to fit through the birth canal. This means that the brain needs time to grow and develop, so humans are born unable to regulate their bodily functions, their behavior, or their emotions. Not yet having a functional cortex for control, communication, and social behavior, babies' brains are preprogrammed to seek out another (right) brain that can help regulate them while their cortex develops. Because the limbic system myelinates early, it has influence during the first year and a half of life, prior to the infant having the cortical development to manage the emotions being generated. During the period of right-hemisphere growth, the right-brain to right-brain interaction with caretakers promotes the development and maintenance of synaptic connections during the establishment of the right brain's functional circuits. One side effect of this process is that a dyadic communication pattern is learned that can serve as a template for relationships throughout life.

Through mirror neurons, the infant signals distress, which evokes a somatic reaction in the caregiver. A bond is formed over time, which involves a process of chemical triggering in both brains, so that responses are not just mirrored but metabolized. This process occurs through eye-to-eye contact (remember the relationship between visual contact and empathy), tactile contact and body gestures, and prosodic verbalizations that induce instant emotional effects in the infant's body. These attunements occur during social engagements; the baby recovers quietly during disengagement while the caretaker looks for reinitiating cues from the baby. Sometimes these attempts to attune have good effects; sometimes the pair is out of sync. If cues are missed or connection does not occur, caretakers can catch it and then repair the interaction. Apparently parents only need 30 percent attunement to have good effects (as long as there is repair), so this becomes a process not only of connection but also of learning to deal with misattunements in relationships. Not only are states of negative arousal modulated, but a model also develops for handling stressful situations. However, if Problems influence this process (caregiver inaccessibility or negative reactions), this could induce enduring negative affect states and bodily responses like the one found in the Still-Face procedure (gaze aversion, sadness, or withdrawal).

And yes, we are talking about attachment, an effect of the biologically based developmental regulation process. Attachment reactions are not fixed or discrete and are nothing more or less than a state of mind. Like most states of mind, different states can be triggered in different settings with different people; there are as many attachment models/states as there are attachment figures. From experience with caregivers, expectations inevitably develop about the availability and responsiveness of others, and these expectations become internal working models of relationships that influence us in interpersonal contexts.

Most of us have heard or read something about the way attachment styles have been categorized. What's interesting to me is how the descriptions relate to the previous discussion about stress and the ANS. Secure attachment appears to correlate with the flexible use of the SES, SNS, and PSNS to handle stress. Through the development of supportive neural structures, a working balance evolves between both parts of the ANS and the right and left brains. Anxious/Ambivalent attachment (occurring in one-eighth of the population) correlates with an overreliance on the hyperactivating SNS and a heightened drive for connection. Under the influence of this model, attempts are made to use the SES by reaching for others, but this reaching does not appear to have a soothing effect. The right brain produces a flood of emotions and memories, with little left-brain balance. The theory is that caregiver responses were likely inconsistent, unreliable, or intrusive.

From my internalized version of my clients:

Clark: My father was highly critical. Now I find that my wife won't be as close to me as I would like. I get really uncomfortable when she doesn't put me or the relationship first. I don't think she really appreciates me and my efforts. I guess I can have strong reactions to her or my son if they don't respond to my liking.

Matt: You think your reactions are strong, Clark? I just say "It's over" to my girlfriend, then apologize and want her to be close.

Avoidant models (affecting one-fifth of the population) have a deactivating effect and result in excessive reliance on the PSNS. These individuals with this style of attachment know they need contact, but as their caregivers were likely underresponsive emotionally, they have no expectations of receiving this contact. They are more oriented to a left-brain linear fashion of operating and so are more emotionally disconnected, generally less lively, and at times dismissing and controlling with peers. Their right brain is typically underdeveloped, so they don't feel their body or their own needs, let alone others' needs:

Doug: I am comfortable without close emotional relationships and would prefer not to depend on others. I feel taken advantage of a lot in relationships. Whatever.

Karen: I am somewhat uncomfortable getting close to others. I want emotionally close relationships, but I find it difficult to trust others completely or to depend on them. I sometimes worry that I will be hurt if I allow myself to become too close to others.

Disorganized models (thankfully more rare) have the effect of creating hyperarousal first (SNS), followed by hypoarousal (PSNS), and often are the effect of developmental trauma. Usually extreme approach-avoidance behavior is involved, shown to and from caregivers, who tend to be frightened or frightening. Individuals with this attachment style tend to have narratives with little coherence, reflecting their lives:

Raymundo: I don't really have anyone. I'm weird, who would like me? I can't stand it when my boss acts like he does, although I do like him. My mom can be so annoying. I have all these health problems. You have all these strange ideas, Jeff.

Like most Narrative Therapists, I don't really like to categorize people or their behavior. Nevertheless, attachment is an important topic in the Interpersonal Neurobiology literature. For me, it is about how much stress is experienced in someone's earliest relationships and the effects of this on later relationships. To return to an earlier concept, this relates to a person's window of tolerance for stress in intimate relationships. The size of this window will determine how quickly someone reacts and experience shapes what form the reaction takes (use SES, SNS, or PSNS), that is, the extent to which Fear/Danger shapes the way someone responds when in close quarters with others. For example, Raymundo can hardly enter into relationships in any manner, Clark and Matt get clingy and demanding, Karen distances, and Doug stays away from actual closeness. They all differ in how quickly and in what conditions a Problem version takes over.

Implicit affect can have a major influence on people's lives, particularly in the way it shapes identities and has effects on relationships. The stress of uncomfortable feelings impacts arousal processes and gets people to react in predictable ways to others around them; helping people anticipate these responses seems to help them manage that arousal. Ultimately, the goal would be to bring this affect into the room and reexperience it with the therapist. In all my years of seeing clients, I have yet to see a couple that was not equally matched on how much Fear was impacting them and their relationship, even if the arousal patterns and responses associated with them seemed very different. It is as if people sense who is safe for them, who will allow them to stay comfortably in their windows.

Thankfully, given the neuroplasticity of the brain and its ability to change with experience, the effects of early experience can be modified. Therapy becomes an opportunity to rewire neural circuitry by providing a different relational experience, one that helps clients shift their relational expectations from danger to comfort. This shift affects the kinds of strategies clients use to manage both relationships and emotions. Bromberg believes that the therapeutic context has a built-in helpful advantage in addressing these issues, because the therapeutic relationship activates the attachment experience, thus facilitating new relational learning. In addition, care responses (from the therapist's vagal system response) reduce stress hormones while activating the SES. Regardless of whether you use the attachment point of view or not, the therapeutic relationship's importance in creating the groundwork for change has been clearly demonstrated.

Back to Raymundo (who was telling me about a visit he had with his mom):

J: Have you had feelings like these before with her?

R: With my mom, you mean?

J: Can you picture being with her as a kid? Let's pick an age . . .

R: I was not protected, no control . . .

J: Where are you feeling those feelings now?

R: In my chest.

J: Stay with those feelings. I know it's hard, they are intense.

R: I'm so uncomfortable at the thought of trying to do things. It's not safe, I'm afraid I will lose control . . . all these negative feelings. I'm afraid I will act on them.

J: (voice cracking) All those strong scary feelings . . . they must be
    so hard to manage when they take over. I know how much you
    want to be cared for.

R: I was kinder to myself when I got sick.

J: (stunned) What was that like for you, to care for yourself in a way
    that gives you the care you deserve?

R: (crying) I was out clothes shopping . . . (He tells a story of wit-
    nessing a mom and her child kindly interacting.)

J: I was imagining that you thought this was important, to give and
    get that kind of care.

R: Yes, it would be nice.

J: What does it say about you, that you wish this for your own life?

*I was working hard to keep the strong feelings in the body, both his and
mine; they were quite intense. I made internalizing comments as opposed
to asking externalizing questions. To help with affect regulation, to use the
therapeutic relationship to help rewire neural structure, I took on the feelings with him. Once they were adequately felt in his body and experienced
in the room with me, I externalized the Problems feeding on the difficult-to-
manage affect. Notice, also, how noncoherent his narrative is, how he jumps
all over the place, how his affect is painful and intrusive. This is common for
those who have experienced developmental trauma. I try to stay very close
to his experience, and somewhat unattached to where I might have wanted
the conversation to go seconds earlier, as anything but a very small step
leads to an experience of misattunement for him.*

Identities II

Let us return to the relationship between identities and dysregulated
affect. We now know that the brain and body react to intolerable affect
(an internal threat) in similar ways as it does to any external threat. We
are wired for an emphasis on safety over cognitive reflection. Bromberg
(2011) suggested that dysregulation is likely occurring when an identity is triggered that we cannot easily manage; the feelings connected to
this identity are activated, influential, and possibly powerful. Neither the
feelings nor the identity is likely preferred. Often this results in a Prob-

lem identity taking over. From a Neuro-Narrative perspective, a Problem identity is a version that manages the Problem-supporting affect and arousal. I imagine we all have experienced one of these popping out and taking over. I previously suggested that different Problems reflect different types of arousal; this holds for the identities that emerge around these Problems. For example, a Trouble-Maker identity reflects attempts to manage escalating decreasing arousal through acting out (triggered if arousal levels are getting too low), while an Overly High-Achieving identity may reflect the use of Obsessiveness and Perfectionism to handle arousal through dampening it down (triggered if arousal levels are getting too high).

These stressful affects with accompanying arousal memories are stored in the lower limbic system, allowing the system to detect unanticipated events that could trigger affect dysregulation. Bromberg (2011) referred to this as the "Shadow of the Tsunami," using this metaphor to represent the internal experience of dysregulated affect. The idea is that we go to some effort to avoid reexperiencing these feelings. Constant vigilance (via neuroception) produces false positives—we overanticipate the same bad thing happening again (those horrible feelings erupting and being painfully unmanageable). One effect of this anticipation is the development of identities to manage these situations, and these identities have real effects on our present interactions.

For example, a client of mine (Andy S, who had worked as a social worker) seemingly could not get a reasonable amount of attention when he was younger and so disconnected from that Really Wanting Attention version because it was so painful. (You could call these wanting-attention feelings decentered but influential.) Now, however, he has a low threshold for not getting his preferences met. In the face of his partner experiencing great distress and requiring attention from him, he loses all empathy and refuses to respond to the distress, telling her he's "not her therapist." His own feelings of not being responded to when he was younger are so powerful, his fear of feeling these unmanageable feelings (affect dysregulation) so strong, and the painful memories of rejection so intense (what happens to us as children is stored with childlike feelings) that he is unable to acknowledge the enormity of his own wants or bring forth the version that is desperate for attention. Instead, an attacking version comes out, not the supportive version I know he would prefer to access at that moment. The attacking version manages the sympathetic arousal he is experiencing. Conflict resolution is made even more difficult as he experiences his partner's experience of him (the attacking version) as "not me," because it is not his intention to respond this way. The kind of responses he then inevitably invites from his partner serves as inadvertent relationship support for the unworthiness that he already feels for not receiving the attention he so desperately wanted. In other words, the only attention he receives is either negative or nonexistent, causing what he fears the most to come true.

Let me try to pull together some of what I have been talking about by way of this example. Consider an identity that did not get enough attention as a child—on a neural level this is a brain state, a state of mind that contains these painful feelings. This identity is potentially invited out by cues that signal a strong need for attention, but because this identity brings with it so much painful feeling, the brain reacts to its emergence as a threat—it is appraised as dangerous by the mind through neuroception. The arousal response associated with the experience, in this case an SNS amping-up response, shapes the version that emerges instead, and out comes an attacking version—a Problem identity. It negatively affects the interaction, acting against the person's preferences about how to treat others.

According to Bromberg (2011), the fear of affect dysregulation (the Shadow of the Tsunami) is shrunk by reliving it in the present and thus making it a cognitive event, stopping the automatic reliance on dissociation as an affective danger detector. Bromberg suggested that, when this occurs, the client can begin to safely distinguish possible overwhelming mental shock from the past and potentially exciting spontaneous interpersonal experiences in the present. The person can become more selective about how to respond, as internal conflict can be borne through easing the mental struggle to hold it cognitively. The person's window of tolerance is enlarged, meaning that the threshold for affective hyperarousal is increased.

Because identities need relationship support to be brought forth, Bromberg (2011) suggested that, while you want therapy to be safe, it can't be too safe, because it is critical to access the stressful affects stored in the limbic system. Michael White used a metaphor of positioning oneself as a therapist as being just behind clients; too far ahead of them pushes them back, and if too far behind, nothing happens. Possibilities for creating a context in which hard-to-acknowledge identities can be safely seen are not restricted to the therapy room; when any kind of personal relationship is operating in a way that allows for use of the SES, it can contain the stressful affects that are involved. For Andy, when these feelings were experienced with me and then got put into words (i.e., narrated), he no longer needed a Problem (SNS-arousal) response to contain them.

What makes it hard, at times, to hold on to preferred identities, especially around someone significant? When we interact with someone, we are interacting with mutual multiple identities. Different identities have different meanings depending on context. A humorous comment may mean a friendly version popped out. In other situations, however, it could mean that a version has popped out that is helping us manage affect, that is responding to arousal levels that are too high or too low for us. A Family Therapy teacher of mine described being determined not to be the one in his family whose function was to deflect the tension, but try as he might, when the tension got unbearable he would tell a funny story. (He explained this from a role in the family perspective, not on the basis of arousal issues and shifts in states of mind as we have been doing.) I imagine we've all had the experience of getting in touch with a memory and feeling overwhelming arousal or a deep, sinking feeling, or perhaps even feeling that way all of a sudden, without knowing why. What versions of ourselves emerge when these feelings take over?

Our internal context can have as much influence as the external one in determining what identities emerge, because either can shape arousal levels. In the therapeutic context, it is mostly about affect that is too high or too low for our particular windows of tolerance (although you saw how I was triggered by Clark's specific self-presentation); with loved ones, the triggers are generally more specific but still tied to arousal tolerance (which determines when and what eventual response occurs). Personally, I have begun to recognize the signs when I am being pulled out of my window in therapy; when the energy in the room is too low for me I revert to my Brooklyn-born talking-too-much version, or I begin to feel sleepy, my mind wanders, and I start to disengage. Sometimes, when the implicit tension in the room gets too high for my particular window, I tell a funny story—this is my Borscht Belt comedian version. Other times I go didactic, perhaps sharing a piece of neurobiology— my teacher version. And sometimes I just find a way to move the session along. Most of the time when I catch myself responding to tension in these ways I switch back, sometimes making it explicit that this has occurred and asking clients what it was like for them during this time. I try to remember that, "The most important source of resistance in the treatment process is the therapist's resistance to what the patient feels" (Paul Russell, quoted in Schore, 2012, p. 132). Next time you find that you have lost your therapist version, feeling a bit frozen or taking over the conversation with one of your stories, it might be useful to consider whether your window of tolerance has been exceeded and use that as helpful information and potential conversation with the client.

That we are multiversioned is good news; ideally we want the flexibility to adjust to any circumstance. In whatever way we nonconsciously appraise the situation to be meaningful (i.e., to have emotional weight to us), we want to be able to switch our internal states fluidly between high-energy (SNS) and low-energy (PSNS) responses to meet environmental changes. We have different versions, different states available to us to manage these different situations.

But what if some of these situations are appraised by us as dangerous in the ways I have been talking about? Then it is likely that less preferred or Problem identities will pop out. Can you feel a nonpreferred identity about to erupt sometimes? I distinguish between two kinds of nonpreferred identities: the nonpreferred Problem one that pops out to manage painful affect, dictated by the embedded arousal response (e.g., Andy S's attacking one), and the really painful identity that lurks in the shadows (e.g., desperately wanting attention and care version).

A Poststructural view allows for all of us to be multiversioned and shaped by dominant discourse. From that point of view, external context determines which version we step into and when. But I now believe that it is not quite that simple: there is an internal context that has to be accounted for as well. As a liberal, white, upper-middle-class, heterosexual man, when do I hold on to my preferred way of interacting with my partner, and when does entitlement take over? I imagine all of us prefer to be emotionally open and receptive to our clients and maximally responsive to our families. These are my preferences, and they happen to dovetail with dominant specifications for men of my social location. But stored affect can dictate which discourse I step into and when, reflexively and without conscious processing. Again, this is to avoid painful versions and is an effect of the arousal I am experiencing.

I have a Not Good Enough version—men tend to be vulnerable to adequacy issues, given their dominant cultural dictates, and I've had my own unique experiences regarding that as well. My Not Good Enough version used to pop out easily with criticism/feedback; now that version has much less strength. If, however, suddenly I'm acting like a real jerk or shutting down, it is likely that I have been triggered into that Not Good Enough version dictated by an implicit emotional response to what is happening at the time. Triggers push us out of one brain state into another. From a physiological standpoint, the arousal responses contained in the emotional memories that are part of that Not Good Enough state help determine whether I am amping up (attacking and acting like a jerk, or using my entitlement to stop the conversation) or, alternatively, damping down (psychically removing myself from the moment when things feel really threatening).

In Narrative Therapy we talk about nonpreferred identities from the position of conscious purpose. I still find this idea quite useful in getting clients to state their preferences and acknowledge the version that they are trying to hold on to. But these versions have already been brought forth, that is, cognitively narrated; other versions, those influenced by implicit affect, have not. These implicit versions nonconsciously encourage responses that do not fit one's preferences. As you have read, basic life stress involves left-brain anxious anticipation and may reflect some danger, but with a larger window of tolerance in which reason still operates. Bigger life threats, which implicit affect can feel like, activate right-brain arousal, and the right brain takes control over the left. We then become reactive to our emotions in ways that deal with this internal threat; when affective intensity exceeds our window of tolerance, the ability to negotiate a preferred identity is gone. And when we are reacting in this manner, our significant others can experience extremes of arousal that influence their ability to hold on to their preferred identity as well. And, whether our triggered response is the same or different from our partner's (SNS vs. PSNS influenced), our windows of tolerance and what triggers us out of them are similar.

Unfortunately, the Narrative strategy of increasing the power held by one version (i.e., building an alternative version/story) does not permanently hold off the Problem identity. Perhaps our client's windows of tolerance become expanded, and it takes more precise triggers, a greater threat, to allow the implicit affect to influence the version we are using to interact with others. The Problem may be suppressed, but the implicit affect will be there lurking, looking for an insuppressible opportunity to pop out and influence situations. At that point it is not a fair fight, because the affect behind these Problem versions becomes active, overriding the preferred versions. This invites the kind of responses from the other that give inadvertent relationship support to the Problem version and likely confirms a Problem version of the other.

For those of you who embraced Family Systems Theory back in the day, we thought of these patterns of responding between partners as complementary (opposite) or symmetrical (similar). Are we now just talking about dynamically oriented defense mechanisms instead (e.g., dissociation and projective identification)? Reviewing the physiologically based wiring behind these responses suggests an alternative understanding, one involving the influence of memories containing a certain type of arousal experience. MRT could make a difference in shifting the arousal responses and conclusions that support the nonpreferred versions, making the Problem version unnecessary. What else might we do as therapists to help?

Enactments Revisited: Working Between the Identities of Client and Therapist

Bromberg (2011), who refers to himself as a neuroanalyst, cautioned against making interpretations, because he believes they make things worse (they are another left-brain intervention for what is a right-brain problem). He pointed instead to the need for affect in order to gain "affective tolerance." In fact, he suggested that enactments (authentic experiential moments between client and therapist) require a personal response. From this point of view, therapist self-disclosure is about sharing our own here-and-now experience, not sharing with the clients similar experiences we may have had. In an enactment, the client's implicit experience is juxtaposed with the therapist's real in-the-MOMENT experience (which might also be implicitly influenced). Schore (2012) agreed that using left-brain conscious verbal strategies is not that useful, because they do not promote myelination of the ventromedial cortex, which controls arousal regulation. He believes that the goal is instead to reexperience dysregulated affect in tolerable doses (i.e., scaffolded) so it can be regulated and integrated.

While the past can be frightening, even in the present, Bromberg (2011) suggested that therapists need to recognize this pain and to care about it, but not experience clients' distress as a message to give up their efforts to bring forth the distress. Working in these windows of tolerance means activating them; how much to activate them and when to repair become a matter of judgment at the time. While the experience of an enactment might find both therapist and client destabilized, hanging in with it will likely result in change. From my perspective, Bromberg is suggesting that, if therapists don't activate these enactments, the effect will instead be an inadvertent reinforcement of the Problem, resulting in a lack of change and more relationship support for the Problem.

Now we have all the pieces we need for the grand finale: a return to the question of what goes into forming new narratives. According to Bromberg (2011), reorganizing internal narratives involves recalling the affects and interpersonal data that had been excluded from the narrative memory of the event as originally reported. He suggested that this recall is invited by the kind of perceptual data I have been referring to that is being enacted between therapist and client. He suggested that the therapeutic relationship itself is drawn into the telling of the narrative, as aspects of the past are being enacted in the here-and-now. *The client's narrative frame is expanded by providing an interpersonal experience that, for all its familiarity, is perceptually different.* Instead of being influenced by all the implicit affect, the affects and events of the past experiences are accessed and available for meaning making and thus for the construction of new narratives. In short, self narratives are expanded through the engagement of previously not symbolized affect, in a co-creative process.

A New Story emerges from the relational experience, one that contains the old, influential feelings now in narrative form:

Therapy = New emotional experiences in the context of a relationship

Summary: Nonconscious Influences

- The body's wired-in response to stress uses arousal patterns to handle dangerous and life-threatening situations. It is an evolutionarily old system; Cozolino (2016) suggested that it is not ideal to manage the demands of today's world.
- Instead of altering affective valence (i.e., whether positive or negative), interventions need to help the client learn to manage different amounts of arousal, because arousal is metabolically costly and fatiguing. One way to know that a person's arousal threshold has been exceeded is that a Problem appears. The process of reexperiencing positive affect (repair) following negative experiences allows clients to learn that negative affect can be tolerated and that relational stress can be handled. This will help them use the SES, which is less biologically costly.
- From a Narrative Therapy perspective, once brought forth and regulated (held by the therapist), affect can then be externalized. Regulation involves monitoring and modifying. If affect remains nonconscious, it can't be modified. Once brought forth into consciousness, the affect can be safely experienced, and the meaning given the experience can be meaningfully externalized. If the Problem has its roots in the past, it was likely a helper at one time but now is having negative effects. The Problem's strategies probably have not changed, just its effects. Once its helpfulness in the past is acknowledged, the real effects of these strategies in the present are more likely to be noticed.
- Unique Outcomes could be thought about as times when a person could have been triggered out of the window of tolerance but wasn't; working on the border of the window offers many possibilities. Increasing the threshold for affective hyperarousal at the edges of regulatory boundaries broadens windows of tolerance.
- For Narrative therapists, decisions about when to bring forth the

Problem (Problem MOMENT) and when to work with developments (UOM) can be made by tracking the client's experience to determine which side of the boundary the client is on. Remember that clients' emotional states in the MOMENT influence what memories are accessible to them.

- In a sense, we are talking about an affective version of Lev Vygotsky's zone of proximal development. For Vygotsky, these were internal developmental processes that require interpersonal interaction to evolve. In this work, what gets scaffolded is not only tolerance of negative affect but also tolerance for positive affect, for novelty, and for uncertainty (e.g., in intimacy situations). What all these situations have in common is the *amount* of arousal they evoke.

- To select and hold on to a preferred identity out of the multiple ones that influence us require not letting these states be chased off by escalating arousal. Expanding our clients' windows of tolerance to be able to tolerate both highs and lows will help them hold on to preferred states. Bringing forth previously nonnarrated affective material and then inviting meaning will make the difference.

- Nonnarrated implicit memories create havoc. Going to Problem MOMENTS or autobiographical MOMENTS can be useful to reenter Problem-supporting memories. For clients who lack access to them, it might be more useful to go to a MOMENT in the session first, to what is happening right now in the therapeutic context: What's it like for you to be with the client? What's it like for the client to be with you?

- Memory Reconsolidation Therapy provides an interesting metamodel for successful therapy of all types. I sometimes pay attention to the MRT formula when organizing my Neuro-Narrative interviews:
  - Bring forth affect-laden critical memories from the past that influence Problems, as well as the conclusions that support Problem identities in the past and present.
  - Juxtapose them with UOMs.
  - Repeat the pairing several times, and invite the client to take a position on the old conclusions and the new ones.
  - Might this three step process be the "ABCs" of therapy?

- Remember to use right-brain strategies for right-brain Problems (e.g., strategies that bring forth and address arousal responses). Cognitive strategies work only for left-brain Problems.
- It is impossible to speak about the client's window of tolerance without discussing the therapist's window of tolerance as well. Working in the manner I have been discussing requires the therapist's ability to stay in a right-brain-dominant state and access embodied intuition, to give personal and not technical responses, and to be able to feel the client's experience and reflect this in nonverbal reactions. White (without ever speaking about it) was a great example of someone who did just that. Remember that enactments require a personal response. My experience is that sharing a personal response (not a conclusion or theory) goes a long way to redressing a power imbalance, especially if shared with an attitude of "this is only my experience, I'm really interested in yours."
- Therapy mirrors the attachment process, because critical relationship factors appear to be more influential than model-specific factors. Attune, attend, and repair if necessary. Remember that human experience shapes neural connections.

Now let's return to Raymundo. After we reviewed the last session, focusing on safety, he brought up the following:

R: I've been concerned about my uncle. I don't think my aunt and mom are taking his problems seriously enough.

J: Tell me about your concerns, Raymundo.

R: I talked with his doctors about his history of heart problems.

J: Can you remember the MOMENT when you decided to care for him?

R: You are always asking me . . . I can't remember.

J: No worries. What was it like for you when I asked you that question?

R: I don't know, frustrating . . .

J: OK, frustrating, so sorry. I feel it too. What was it like for you to decide to care for your uncle?

R: I'm not sure. It's all painful.

J: (voice lowered) Can you tell me more about all this pain, Raymundo?

R: It's unsettling, like when I was a little kid with my mom.

J: Where is the unsettled feeling in your body?

R: Here (pointing) . . . *pain* . . . not safe . . .

J: What happens to you when that Not Safe feeling is around?

R: I want to get away . . . those angry feelings. Why can't I be normal?

J: (not accepting the invitation to go to that self-narrative) How else do these Not Safe feelings affect you?

R: I'm anxious, on guard.

J: I imagine it's so difficult for you. Are you feeling those feelings right now?

R: It's hard to feel them . . . some tension . . . critical thoughts . . . I need distance.

J: Can you hang in there a bit longer with them? What else do Not Safe feelings do to you?

R: I can't deal with the complexity of people (seemingly getting this for the first time). I just wish for protection.

J: Go ahead and imagine someone protecting you. What comes up?

R: Joy . . . you know I called an old high school friend for the first time in years. He's not perfect . . . but I was his best friend. I remembered him while talking with my mom last week. It felt good to talk with him.

J: Wow, this seems like a step toward safety to me. What was it like for you?

R: I felt comfort.

J: It seems to me that there is loneliness in your life . . . I feel it.

R: I am lonely, I realize I want to be around other people. I also talked to a professor friend. I shared some of my circumstance with him. He was nice to me.

J: It appears that you have been taking these steps, these steps to connect with others. What's helping you to do this?

R: I *do* enjoy other people . . . yeah. If I feel strong about myself, I am more accepting of others.

J: Enjoying others, feeling strong about yourself and accepting others. Would these things contribute to safety then?

R: (smiling) I even had an OK conversation with a coworker.

J: If it's all right with you, I'd like to hear more about this. Can we go through the MOMENT in some detail?

Raymundo describes the MOMENT. When he finishes:

J: What's in your body as you are sharing this with me?

R: Capable . . . younger.

J: What else?

R: Safety . . .

From my point of view, there were a couple of interesting turning points in this interview. The first was when I attempted to invite Raymundo into a MOMENT and he couldn't accept this invitation. My assumption when this occurs is that strong feelings have been activated, and the body perceives a threat. When I get a response like this, I also try to remember that, for some, what I am attempting to invite is material that has not yet really been narrated, that I am inviting the client into a new experience, one that is likely quite scary, uncomfortable, and without cognitive structure. After he turned down my invitation, then you saw me switch to the present, to what was happening between Raymundo and me: "What was it like for you when I asked you that question?" I attended to the feelings we both were experiencing in that MOMENT, to the enacted experience. I then asked a more scaffolded question: "What was it like for you to decide to care for your uncle?" This question didn't require as much affective involvement. All the while I was attending to the affective experiences emerging in the conversation.

You can see how asking the question "What's it like?" enabled Raymundo to note his experience in the version he was able to be in with me and that eventually this allowed him to get in touch with the threatening material from the past. Asking this question allows the experience in the present and memories of the past to be held simultaneously in working memory, thereby bypassing the amygdala's interference with hippocampal functioning, eventually allowing the client's experience to become consciously available for narration. You can see how the material from the past became available to us in the session: "It's unsettling, like when I was a little kid with my mom."

The second turning point was when I was able to turn down his invitation to go to his Problem-influenced narrative: "Why can't I be normal?" I stayed with inviting out the affective effects in a very Narrative manner: "How else do these Not Safe feelings affect you?" Going to the identity conclusions at that time (not normal) would have provided inadvertent relational support for the Problem, which would have kept him from experiencing all these difficult feelings. He allowed me to turn down this invitation; once I did so, and he was able to bring forth terrified feelings, hang in there with them, feel them, and manage them (with my help), he was able to come to a stunning (for him) realization: "I can't deal with the complexity of people . . . I just wish for protection." And once that occurred, he had access (again, with the help of my questions) to some steps he had made, to which I was able to invite new meaning. You may recall the ABCs of therapy from the summary section.

I was also able to address my experience of his experience of loneliness for the first time. It just came to me in that MOMENT (a right-brain to right-brain communication). I realized I was afraid to acknowledge this previously, that maybe it would have been too much for him. As I write this, a little voice in my head wonders, too much for whom? Was this an example of my tendency to tread a little lightly? In this case, I don't think so.

Coda

Pathways of Power:
Questions for Jeff From the Iron Throne

> *In its function, the power to punish is not essentially different from that of curing or educating.*
> —Michel Foucault (1977)

> *Tread lightly.*
> —Walter White (2012)

> *When you play the game of thrones, you win or you die. There is no middle ground.*
> —Cersei Lannister (2011)

This section raises critical questions pertinent to the integration of Neuro with Narrative Therapy. Narrative Therapists are very fond of asking questions, so I structured this last section accordingly. In a sense, it is as if I am being interviewed by someone that is influenced by the understandings of my pre-Neuro self. I hope that these would be questions that you, the reader, might ask, especially if you are coming from a purely Narrative perspective.

*Let's start with a few warm-up questions before bringing forth the
thorny issues related to power. First, why write this book?*

I am hoping my work (and this book) will contribute to help opening up
Narrative Therapy to a whole new set of possibilities. I believe we need to
be more open to continue to grow and evolve; openness to new possibilities is how systems change. Without change, without being responsive
to the demands of the current cultural context, systems tend to die out.
Some of this change needs to be on a meta-level, an evolution of ideo-
logical structures to account for the integration of new ideas. Perhaps
this will come in the form of a meta-structure of overarching ideas that
encompass Narrative, Neuro, and whatever else will help address the
Problems of the day.

*How have these ideas been received by those who maintain a firm
grip on Narrative's foundational structures?*

There seemed to be resistance—many long-established Narrative Therapists didn't seem happy about my new direction. Stephen Madigan, who
has always been supportive of my work, suggested it was because there
was a difference in meaning, each not knowing what the other was trying
to say (personal communication, 2017). Nevertheless, I hope that Narrative Therapy is still about *the real effects of an idea* or practice, not about
some ideas being good or correct and others being bad or wrong. Is there
now an immutable dominant discourse of Narrative Therapy? Whatever
the case, I do prefer being out on the edge, pushing the boundaries. For
some, that's where it all started.

After reading the dialogues, can I expect to just jump into the work?

Not yet—first you must confront strong affect! It's not been easy for me
to get to the place where the work you see currently resides. My changes
in thinking have resulted in inevitable growing pains. In the beginning,
it felt like the old me as a therapist was dead and that I was walking
through sessions in a liminal fog. I actually asked people how they were
feeling, a question I had not asked in almost forty years as a therapist.
I was frightened; it took me a while to get the point here: bodily based
emotions are our primary expressions of experience, and it is useful
to have these expressed directly and congruently in the room. It's not

always easy. Integrating them into the work, in both conscious and non-conscious form, is the challenge.

Are you still a Narrative Therapist?

Yes, I am still a Narrative Therapist. I use a Narrative Therapy structure for my conversations. Primarily through asking questions, I externalize Problems and look for Unique Outcomes (preferably MOMENTS). I am very interested in the sociopolitical context that Problems live in. I don't see my clients as separate from me in that we all have lives where we struggle and succeed. But I also use a neurobiological lens, with all the different possibilities it brings for regarding the Problem and for guiding important therapeutic tasks. My favorite metaphor is "jamming": musical groups that jam depart from the initial threads and themes of the musical conversation into music that is co-created by the group members in the MOMENT, exploring and reaching in other directions before returning to the original starting point. Jam rock is an example of this type of playing. Indian music does this as well, and as I happily discovered when looking up references for this book, Michael White (2011) pointed to jazz music as a metaphor for co-creation. In my work, I go off into different realms of ideas before coming back to Narrative ideas and practices as a central organizing theme. Specifically, Narrative and Poststructural viewpoints provide a general metastructure, from which I feel free to bring in other possibilities, other areas of conversation to take up in my Narrative structure. While the ideas come from both Structural and Poststructural places, relational thinking becomes a specific metastructure that is consonant with both Narrative Therapy and Interpersonal Neurobiology. So does seeing clients as people whose preferred identity is potentially separate from the influence of their bodily based emotions and the knowledge and practices these influence. Maybe we can refer to this meta place as pan-structural.

Can we revisit the question of affect?

Sure. In my many years of engaging in traditional Narrative conversations, my attempt to stay focused on my clients' experiences (or to create experiences in training groups) was generally done without specific regard for the amount of emotion these experiences evoked. I then began to be struck by how important and useful affect is to the equation. Most therapists think this is a no-brainer, despite some not necessarily having an idea about what this means to their work, other than the importance of talking about "feelings." I finally got that the whole point is for clients to actually experience the feelings in the room with the therapist, and not just talk about them. Consistent with my personal experience, I believe that it helps for therapists to experience these feelings as well. Once felt by the therapist, the response back to the client comes from an embodied position, one more likely to feel "genuine" to the client, as it is taken up as part of right-brain to right-brain communication—a nonconscious experience. Feeling it in the body also helps therapists see more clearly how their next question is being influenced by their own experience, and perhaps more easily monitor if the question that pops into their head relates more to the client's experience or to their own. We are changed by our interactions with our clients; it's helpful to more directly and consciously notice how this process evolves.

If clients talked, what might they say were turning points in their work with you?

It would be interesting to ask them that question, but from my point of view it seemed that when I stepped out of traditional Narrative work and into some of the possibilities I summarize in Chapters 3–6, they began to report and show more movement in the directions they wanted to go.

For Matt, Narrative work set a direction, but addressing the influence of old implicit affect and the meaning it created for him was critical to his being able to manage the Problem. In his key interpersonal interactions with his girlfriends, these Problem-influenced meanings/conclusions about himself weren't what he experienced; it was just the terrifying affect that had real effects on his reactivity. Using MOMENTS made an immediate difference to the conversation becoming emotion filled.

Doug was not able to engage in meaning-full conversations without a lot of help. Breathing, picturing, embodying, and mindfulness meditation had the effect of allowing for Narrative conversations that were actually filled with narratives instead of just left-brain rhetoric. Using these practices dramatically changed Doug's ability to access the Problem.

Karen is terrified by strong affect, because it brought up her painful feelings of being very small. She would prefer to hang in there with Clark, but when the affective intensity reached a certain point she couldn't. By bringing forth critical Problem memories containing strong implicit affect, her window for affective tolerance was greatly enlarged.

Clark had a version that was hard to access because it came with affect that was really frightening. In that version, he was useless and not capable. A Problem version popped out to manage this painful one, getting him to respond in ways that were completely antithetical to his conscious purposes. I could access this version only by sharing my experiences in the MOMENT with him, as none of the above is intended by him. Once in the in-session MOMENT, Clark's preferred version was more accessible.

For Raymundo, most of the time even Unique Outcomes or Unique Outcome MOMENTS brought forth more affect than he could handle. I had to follow him really carefully and invite out the affect associated with his preferred version very slowly. The same goes for the affect associated with the little boy who was frightened all the time and very wary of others. Affect, then meaning, works really well; developmental trauma makes doing this challenging, as enactments occur at a high frequency and intensity.

What about you?

For me, engaging in mindfulness meditation and then picturing the Problem was very helpful. Working to revise my relationship to the Problem during the meditations made a huge difference to finishing this book. I also engaged in a daily meditation practice to help me to manage Anxiety that took over when my increasingly serious visual difficulties made it difficult to read and focus.

Thinking about my work with these clients, and with myself, one reflection I have concerns the relationship between Unfelt Anxiety and Avoidance. I agree with Philip Bromberg that we are especially prone to Problems (in this case Avoidance) when an old identity threatens to pop out and we don't want to feel the feelings associated with it. Whether you think of this as an effect of a Problem identity or just as an effect of having to do something that brings up Fear/Anxiety, Avoidance uses this energy to move us away from our preferred directions into ones that have bad effects. It does feel like a relief when the Avoidance makes the Anxiety go away, but it's a Devil's pact. That's what makes going to that affect-filled MOMENT so useful.

Can the process of Narrative Therapy facilitate affect management?

In effect, yes. While it does not address this issue directly, traditional Narrative Therapy sometimes accomplishes affect management, in several ways.

First, Narrative Therapy focuses the therapist on the experience of the client. While this focus is not on affect explicitly, affect might be implicitly addressed, depending on the client, therapist, and Problem. The same might be said for how much the therapist is attuned to the client; ideally the practice of following the client's experience will construct a level of interpersonal involvement. Whether this attunement will regularly develop into full-blown resonance depends even more on the therapist's openness and relationship to his or her own body, allowing a felt sense of what the two right brains are communicating. It is also my experience that resonance can occur spontaneously through a real coherence that can happen between any two people. Michael White spoke of "transport" to describe the potential experience of Outsider Witness group members when listening to a client's story; I believe that he was getting at a similar phenomena. Once team members are transported, their response to the client very likely captures the client's affect. Attunement connects the therapist to the client in a way that makes the client's affect seem more manageable; resonance/transport does so even more.

Second, some therapists intuitively follow the affect in the room; White was a master at doing this. Following the affect makes it feel more manageable to the client. Third, Narrative questions can both capture affect and begin the process of linking it with cognitive structure. Questions that intuitively emerge when the therapeutic process involves attunement and resonance have a higher likelihood of bringing forth the relevant affect, making it more likely that it will be linked to cognitive structures that make sense to the client. Ultimately, externalizing Problems mirrors neurobiologists' idea that naming the Problem tames the affect generated by the limbic firing associated with the Problem. Externalization is an extremely effective affect management strategy when Problems are named in a way that links them to affective experience (whether this is done by the therapist explicitly or inadvertently).

Now to get to "power": are you concerned about the effects of using the therapeutic relationship to directly facilitate affect management?
I hope that, at this point in the book, it is needless to say that being mindful about affect while in the room would allow all of the above to happen with conscious purpose. I imagine that it would be more palatable to Narrative Therapists to have affect regulation occur through the effects of the work, rather than through therapists centering themselves and using the therapeutic relationship to do it more explicitly. I am well aware of the concern that the latter way of going about it might put the therapist in a position of too much power in the client's life and can center the therapeutic relationship in a way that moves other relationships into lesser positions.

In what ways does going about the work in a purely decentered way have the effect of flattening out the power relationship? Like it or not, clients are usually clear that the therapist is important to them, both in the present and in the future. I believe that this is inevitable, that any significant relationship has lasting effects, that relationships that directly or indirectly foster a rich attachment are recognized by the brain as especially meaningful. Much to my chagrin (at least back in the day), when I have reviewed my work with clients at the end of the therapy and asked about what was most helpful, more often than not they said something about the importance of me to them, and not about my interesting, creative Narrative practices.

This is consistent with what we know from psychotherapy outcome research findings, that the therapeutic relationship is more important to outcome than any model-specific effects. Indeed, my personal experience has been that I had the same amount of success using any model of therapy (although I have enjoyed doing Narrative Therapy the most, because it is consistent with my politics and with the values I hold about how to understand and interact with others). My fantasy is that White was always very successful as well, even before Narrative Therapy. This is not to say that there is something magical about Michael White (or me, or you). It likely has to do with the way we have always interacted with our clients despite whatever model we thought we were using.

What does it take to stay accountable to the effects of being in a position of power with your clients?

Therapists become an important part of the membered team that supports a client's preferred direction. It is our responsibility, however, to make sure that our conversation elevates other relationships and other people in our clients' lives into even more important positions on this team. Nevertheless, I still believe it is good therapeutic practice to make use of the important relationship between therapist and client directly in the work, all the while attending to the real effects of doing so, and consulting with our clients about what is happening between us. As I discussed when deconstructing some of my conversation with Matt, heightening the internalization of affect before externalizing it likely has different effects on the relationship than going more directly to externalization. It is also important to make sure that the conversation moves in the direction of translating the developments in therapy to relationships outside the therapy. Once safety is experienced in the relationship, it actually makes it easier for clients to access other experiences, both the ones that were frightening and the ones that have provided safety in their lives.

To continue with this theme, what are the implications of the questions you raised for therapists in Chapter 4, in the section titled "What About Us?" Are you speaking about therapists' accountability or responsibility in their position in their clients' lives in some new ways?

Yes. What I now aspire to from an accountability/responsibility standpoint has evolved in a broader way. Previously, I understood accountability primarily as therapists being subject to the effects of whatever they said or did, regardless of their intentions. Specifically, these effects involved the experience of the client. Now I understand my responsibilities to also include being maximally emotionally available to my clients, in both mind and body. In my case, thirty minutes daily of mindful meditation keeps me open in these ways; I see it as the workout I need to do to perform at my best professionally (and personally as well).

Am I being a bit prescriptive? I imagine so. But if, as White suggested, Narrative Therapy is definitely not about "anything goes" and all about "nothing goes," that all ideas and practices are accountable to their effects, then I am comfortable with strongly suggesting that therapists should develop a mindfulness meditation practice. In my experience, the effects of my meditation practice far exceed anything else I know for helping me have a mind that's available to other minds. Meditation also facilitates tracking and handling difficult affect, another area I believe is useful for therapeutic work. Mindfulness meditation helps me get a look at my windows of tolerance for highs and lows, the signs that I have been invited out of them, and what to do when this occurs.

The same is true in recommending this idea to my clients; I am pretty confident in the effects it will have for them. The difficult issue here, from a Narrative perspective, stems once again from the concern that recommendations coming from someone in a position of power could be experienced as mandates to those in lesser positions of power, as they might feel these are prescriptions for their lives they can't or shouldn't turn down. I believe that it's all in the delivery; my medical doctor may tell me what I should do, but even from him I experience it as different when he frames it as a possibility that might be useful to me, subject to my personal decisions and preferences. I do believe we have to pay attention to how we share any idea with our clients; this includes what we might see or how we might feel about anything. Keeping comments in the subjunctive, as possibilities, is critical across the board. I like to be curious about what my clients think about anything I say, and to be curious about the effects afterward about anything they enter into that I might have influenced.

I guess therapy can't be neutral. Can we avoid being in a position of power?
It's a nice fantasy. As Bill O'Hanlon, renowned Eriksonian therapist, flippantly suggested many years ago, to deal in ideas such as this: maybe you should lie down on a couch until it goes away.

All right. Then aren't you using your position of power to influence constructions that are important to Narrative Therapists? Specifically, aren't you really returning us back to yesteryear, particularly with respect to blaming parents for Problems from the past?

Early experience has an influence on developing brains; early in life neural tracks are being laid down between the limbic system and the right brain. Through the ways they interact with the child, all caretakers are, inadvertently or not, preparing children for appreciating and managing the dangers of the world in the unique ways that the caretakers understand them. This includes how to handle interpersonal stress, what to consider dangerous, and what kind of response mediated by the autonomic nervous system is useful. In the same sense, most parents are well intentioned and love their children; they deserve better than to be pathologized by well-meaning therapists. How do we address effects without pointing the finger unhelpfully at who and what contributed to the Problem? No doubt, the argument is complex. Nikolas Rose and Joelle Abi-Rached questioned why our field keeps coming back to "managing parents in the name of the formation of good citizens" (2013, p. 196), instead of addressing larger social Problems (e.g., poverty, social inequalities). They see Neuro as being only the most recent example of putting the focus on parents and the family. Yet, while parents' minds are shaped by culture, given the influential position parents are in, their minds also inform the direction that the culture takes. Minds evolve in a cultural context and then shape the context.

Regardless of all the possible different theoretical vantage points, what we work with in the room is constituted by how our clients' experiences have been previously shaped and stored in memory, and the conclusions drawn from these experiences. Yes, we can deconstruct these experiences along dominant cultural lines, and this can shift meaning. But what is locked in those "special synapses" I wrote about in Chapter 6 is strong affect, often related to experiences in which parents played a central role. In the end, this affect will always have a strong influence on how people are living their lives and the conclusions they hold about themselves and others.

Is resistance indeed futile?

It is important to note that Neuro is very clear that, given neuroplasticity, the brain can *always* be changed through experience. This includes the experiences accrued with parents at different times in our lives. Richard Davidson and Sharon Begley (2012) discussed a series of studies by Michael Meaney that demonstrate how experience can affect the way a gene gets expressed. Offspring of "anxious" rats were switched with offspring of calm rats; the rats raised by the responsive, nurturing rats turned out calm despite their genetic backgrounds; the ones with a calm background raised by anxious rats turned out otherwise. Most interesting, not only were the calming effects due to direct nurturing, but also the nurturing experience influenced gene expression: fewer stress hormone receptors were produced in the young rats' brains; consequently, they produced lower levels of stress hormones and so behaved more calmly. The relationship between nature and nurture is indeed complex.

Despite the theoretical and ethical importance of this debate, what stands out most for me is my experience in the room with clients. What I know from this is that when Problem-supporting stored affect is brought forth and into the client's body, all of a sudden (complications from developmental trauma aside), what was a thin, Problem-influenced description of parents turns into a bigger, thicker picture, where Problems are put in perspective and other experiences with parents, not just Problem-influenced ones, are noticed. I don't lead with a parent question; I just ask about familiarity of experience. Matt is an excellent example of what I am talking about. Doug and Karen love their parents and see them as separate from the Problems their parents participated in. I truly believe that when Clark lets someone help him with this parent issue, his perspective will widen. Even Raymundo has occasional times when he can get in touch with loving MOMENTS with his mom.

What happened to conscious purpose? Why is this so important to the questions about power?

This is the thorniest question of them all: how to balance conscious purpose with nonconscious influences. I like the term *nonconscious* because it doesn't come with the meaningful history associated with *unconscious*, a word that conjures an image of an all-knowing therapist who under-stands more about their patients' "reality" than the patients can know in their own minds. Working the way I do now, that picture couldn't be further from my truth. I hope readers can tell this from the dialogues in this book. As it always was in my work, everything is co-created and evolves from a conversation that follows the client's experience.

What makes you think you can make the not known, known?
I hope it is also clear, in these discussions about memories and stress, and nonconscious stressful affects contained in these memories, that what I am talking about are biologically based arousal responses that are triggered in times of threat and then need to be somehow managed. Are these even knowable unless they are triggered? All of a sudden the person is flooded with affect and reactive to the current situation. When lying dormant, like a sleeping snake in the grass, this affect is usually not seen or felt—this allows us to move forward in life. When I purposefully solicit MOMENTS with clients, these bring affect with them, which can trigger times clients felt similarly. Because emotions focus us, they also create a purpose, to attend to what is being felt, and this makes remem-bering past experiences more likely. How conscious is this purpose?

As I have described in this book, memory affects probability by mak-ing some experiences more likely to occur than others. Gregory Bateson (1972) suggested a similar idea when he stated that a cybernetic expla-nation is negative, that what occurs does so because other things are restrained from occurring, thereby changing the probabilities. In his concept of mind he used the analogy of watching an event on televi-sion and wanting additional coverage, how that would require extra cir-cuitry, in effect decreasing the range of what you could find out—each step of increased consciousness in one part will reduce the total amount of available consciousness. One could understand memories from the perspective of restraints, in that much of our self-identity is governed by processes that are nonconscious. Again, this is necessary, allowing us to be functional and respond at the time to what we experience. Otherwise, we would hardly be efficient enough to deal with the world and survive.

According to Bateson, we see an "unconsciously" edited version of what we perceive, where the specifics are guided by our purposes. These purposes get the information we need for handling things but don't always give us information about the entire system. He described this as a shortcut but suggested that it does not allow for maximum wisdom. From a Neuro perspective, we could describe this in terms of left-brain and right-brain functions. I hope the difference here between left-brain- and right-brain-managed stress was clear; only the former is easily accessed consciously and amenable to cognitively oriented interventions. Bateson seems to caution that a focus on conscious purpose can upset the balance by not giving us the total picture, and that the solution lies with the individual having access to more of the total mind. He believed that accessing the "unconscious" is required for the whole to be known better, and that what is needed is a synthesis of both parts. I believe that the kind of interviewing you read in this book about accomplishes this synthesis.

It's a question of balance. Would it be helpful to you for the nonconscious to be made conscious? Wouldn't you prefer to know something about what your nonconscious influences are, for them to be made conscious? In Chapter 5 I asked Karen to continue to notice what happens when the Problem enters her body, how it takes her away from what she wants and allows the "Smallness" to get what it wants instead. This bifurcated question essentially juxtaposed Karen's conscious purpose with the nonconscious direction the Problem took her in. Karen wanted to have an enduring connection with Clark, while the Smallness wanted her to be frightened about the potential loss of self this might bring. And no amount of conscious purpose helped Clark hold on to his preferred way of being with Karen, when the arousal he experienced was too much for him to manage. Ironically, this could occur when issues regarding his son's welfare came up; these were so important to him that all his care and competency came into play, and this opened the door for the old version of him to create havoc.

With certain triggers, Anxiety is too big; might you want to know what has that kind of potential influence? We know that alternative stories don't take away the potential influence of Problem stories when presented with certain triggers. I gave the example earlier where even White (2011) described how someone whom he was consulting with had images from the past that were influencing responses to clients. Madigan (personal communication, 2017) shared with me that, on a tape he had viewed, White said that the nonconscious was a frontier that Narrative needed to address.

Resistance is futile part II: what about free will?

No doubt that the question of what influences conscious preferences is difficult. How much does the influence of Anxiety memories serve as a restraint on other choices, other preferences, making some choices more probable than others? Externalizing the Anxiety opens space to notice other possibilities, as long as the affect is brought forth and managed (yes, I have said that before). Questions that follow the affect will also inevitably be following that which motivates the client most, to do more or less of something that may or may not be supporting the client's conscious purposes.

In the end, whatever the case is here, my understanding of this issue is that working with conscious purpose keeps the conversation centered on the client's "lived experience" and not on the therapist's imagination. I am all for this; I just think we could center the conversation on the client and hold on to our imagination about what might be influencing the client as well. I hope the dialogues in this book reflect this both-and position.

Is there a middle ground?

Yes, I believe so. I hope I've been hovering around it. In the end, my clients have the final word on this matter as well.

Afterword

Possibilities and Future Jamming

> *Because this is how we survive. We tell our-*
> *selves . . . that we are the walking dead.*
> —Rick Grimes

> *People can try and set you in the right direction,*
> *but they can't show you the way.*
> —Morgan Jones

Did you enjoy the ride? I hope so, and I hope that you found some useful ideas and practices to take into your own work or pursue in your own studies. And that the work you will do as a result of incorporating new possibilities will add to the possibilities for Narrative work in general. It is exciting to me to imagine you taking ideas from neurobiology and developing Narrative practices to address them!

For those readers coming from Neuro and not Narrative, I hope it was not too simplistic; as I set out to keep the Neuro light. Indeed, I purposely avoided saying too much about specific brain structure and function, because I didn't think it would be helpful to this conversation. I also didn't directly address the important topic of integration.

Nevertheless, on a process level, I hope that I honored integration by first differentiating Neuro and Narrative and then linking them together.

I'd be curious to hear what you think about all of this, perhaps at a conference or by e-mail.

—Jeff

References

Angus, L. E., & Greenberg, L. S. (2011). *Working with narrative in emotion-focused therapy: Changing stories, healing lives.* Washington, DC: American Psychological Association.

Armstrong, C. (2015). Creative memory reconsolidation. In M. Dahlitz & G. Hall (Eds.), *Memory reconsolidation in psychotherapy: The Neuropsychotherapist special issue* (pp. 79–93). Park Ridge, Australia: Neuropsychotherapist.

Bateson, G. (1972). *Steps to an ecology of mind: Collected essays in anthropology, psychiatry, evolution, and epistemology.* San Francisco, CA: Chandler.

Beaudoin, M. N., & Zimmerman, J. (2011). Narrative therapy and interpersonal neurobiology: Revisiting classic practices, developing new emphases. *Journal of Systemic Therapies, 30*(1), 1–13.

Beels, C. C. (2009). Some historical conditions of narrative work. *Family Process, 48,* 363–378.

Bromberg, P. (2011). *The shadow of the tsunami and the growth of the relational mind.* New York, NY: Routledge.

Brown, R. P., & Gerbarg, P. L. (2012). *The healing power of the breath: Simple techniques to reduce stress and anxiety, enhance concentration, and balance your emotions.* Boston, MA: Shambhala.

Bruner, J. S. (1986). *Actual minds, possible worlds.* Cambridge, MA: Harvard University Press.

Bruner, J. S. (1990). *Acts of meaning.* Cambridge, MA: Harvard University Press.

Cozolino, L. (2016). *Why therapy works: Using our minds to change our brains.* New York, NY: W. W. Norton.

Dammbeck, L. (2003). Heinz von Foerster interview. In *Das Netz.* Lutz Dammbeck Filmproduktion, Südwestrundfunk (SWR).

Davidson, R. J., & Begley, S. (2012). *The emotional life of your brain: How its unique patterns affect the way you think, feel, and live—And how you can change them.* London: Penguin.

Ecker, B. (2015a). Memory reconsolidation understood and misunderstood. *International Journal of Neuropsychotherapy, 3*(1), 2–46.

Ecker, B. (2015b). A primer on memory reconsolidation and its psychotherapeutic use as a core process of profound change. In M. Dahlitz & G. Hall (Eds.), *Memory reconsolidation in psychotherapy: The Neuropsychotherapist special issue* (pp. 69–78). Park Ridge, Australia: The Neuropsychotherapist.

Ecker, B. (2015c). Using NLP for memory reconsolidation. In M. Dahlitz & G. Hall (Eds.), *Memory reconsolidation in psychotherapy: The Neuropsychotherapist special issue* (pp. 69–78). Park Ridge, Australia: The Neuropsychotherapist.

Ecker, B., Ticic, R., & Hulley, L. (2012). *Unlocking the emotional brain: Eliminating symptoms at their roots using memory reconsolidation.* New York, NY: Routledge.

Epston, D. (2014). Keynote address presented at the Narrative Therapy and Community Work Conference, Adelaide, South Australia.

Epston, D., White, M., & Murray, K. (1993). A proposal for a re-authoring therapy: Rose's revisioning of her life and a commentary. In S. McNamee & K. J. Gergen (Eds.), *Therapy as social construction* (pp. 96–115). London: Sage.

Fishbane, M. (2007). Wired to connect: Neuroscience, relationships, and therapy. *Family Process, 46*(3), 395–412.

Fishbane, M. (2013). *Loving with the brain in mind.* New York, NY: W. W. Norton.

Fosha, D. (2013). Turbocharging the affects of innate healing and redressing the evolutionary tilt. In D. J. Siegel, & M. Solomon (Eds.), *Healing moments in psychotherapy: Affective neuroscience, development, and clinical practice* (pp. 129–168). New York, NY: W. W. Norton.

Foucault, M. (1977). *Discipline and punish: The birth of the prison.* (A. Sheridan, Trans.). London: Allen Lane, Penguin. (Original work published 1975.)

Foucault, M. (1980). *Power/knowledge: Selected interviews and other writings.* New York, NY: Pantheon.

Foucault, M. (1982). The subject and power. In H. Dreyfus & P. Rabinow (Eds.), *Michel Foucault: Beyond structuralism and hermeneutics* (pp. 208–226). Brighton, UK: Harvester.

Geertz, C. (1973). Thick description: Toward an interpretive theory of culture. In *The interpretation of cultures: Selected essays* (pp. 3–30). New York, NY: Basic Books.

. Geertz, C. (1986). Making experiences, authoring selves, in V. Turner and E. Bruner (Eds.), *The anthropology of experience.* (pp. 373–380). Chicago, IL: University of Illinois Press.

Geller, S. M., & Porges, S. W. (2014). Therapeutic presence: Neurophysiological mechanisms mediating feeling safe in therapeutic relationships. *Journal of Psychotherapy Integration, 24*(3), 178–192.

Gergen, K. J. (1985). The social constructionist movement in modern psychology. *Modern Psychologist, 40*, 266–275.

Goldman, R. N., & Greenberg, L. (2013). Working with identity and self-soothing in emotion-focused therapy for couples. *Family Process, 52*(1), 62–82.

Gottman, J., & Levenson, R. (1986). Assessing the role of emotion in marriage. *Behavioral Assessment, 8*(1), 31–48.

Greenberg, L., & Johnson, S. (1986). Affect in marital therapy. *Journal of Marital and Family Therapy, 12*(1), 1–10.

Guilfoyle, M. (2009). Theorizing relational possibilities in narrative therapy. *Journal of Systemic Therapies, 28*(2), 19–33.

Hanson, R. (2013). *Hardwiring happiness: The new brain science of contentment, calm, and confidence.* New York, NY: Harmony Books.

Hebb, D. O. (1949). *The organization of behavior.* New York, NY: Wiley.

Iacoboni, M., Molnar-Szakacs, I., Gallese, V., Buccino, G., Mazziotta, J. C., & Rizzolatti, G. (2005). Grasping the intentions of others with one's own mirror neuron system. *PLoS Biology 3*(3): e79. http://dx.doi.org/10.1371/journal.pbio.0030079.

Johnson, S., & Greenberg, L. (1987). Emotionally focused marital therapy: An overview. *Psychotherapy: Theory, Research, Practice, Training Special Issue: Psychotherapy with Families, 24*(3 Suppl.), 552–560.

Kabat-Zinn, J. (2003). *Coming to our senses.* New York, NY: W. W. Norton.

Konrath, S. H., O'Brien, E. H., & Hsing, C. (2011). Changes in dispositional empathy in American college students over time: A meta-analysis. *Personality and Social Psychology Review, 15*(2), 180–198.

Lanius, R. A., Bluhm, R., & Frewen, P. A. (2013). A window into the brain of complex PTSD: Clinical and neurobiological perspectives. In D. J. Siegel & M. Solomon (Eds.), *Healing moments in psychotherapy* (pp. 49–66). New York, NY: W. W. Norton.

Lazar, S. W., Kerr, C. E., Wasserman, R. H., Gray, J. R., Greve, D. N., Treadway, M. T., McGarvey, M., Quinn, B. T., Dusek, J. A., Benson, H., Rauch, S. L., Moore, C. L. et al. (2005). Meditation experience is associated with increased cortical thickness. *NeuroReport, 16*(17), 1893–1897.

LeDoux, J. E. (1996). *The emotional brain.* New York, NY: Simon and Schuster.

LeDoux, J. E. (2002). *Synaptic self: How our brains become who we are.* New York, NY: Penguin.

Levitin, D. J. (2006). *This is your brain on music: The science of a human obsession.* New York, NY: Penguin.

Madigan, S. (2011). *Narrative therapy.* Washington, DC: American Psychological Association.

Marlatt, G. A. (2006). Mindfulness meditation: Reflections from a personal journey. *Current Psychology, 25,* 155–172.

McGilchrist, I. (2009). *The master and the emissary: The divided brain and the making of the Western world.* New Haven, CT: Yale University Press.

McGilchrist, I. (2013). Hemisphere differences and their relevance to psychotherapy. In D. J. Siegel & M. Solomon (Eds.), *Healing moments in psychotherapy* (pp. 67–88). New York, NY: W. W. Norton.

Montgomery, A. (2013). *Neurobiology essentials for clinicians.* New York, NY: W. W. Norton.

Myerhoff, B. (1982). Life history among the elderly: Performance, visibility and remembering. In J. Ruby (Ed.), *A crack in the mirror: Reflexive perspectives in anthropology* (pp. 99–118). Philadelphia, PA: University of Pennsylvania Press.

Ogden, P. (2009). Emotion, mindfulness, and movement: Expanding the regulatory boundaries of the window of affect tolerance. In D. Fosha, D. J. Siegel, & M. Solomon (Eds.), *The healing power of emotion: Affective neuroscience, development, and clinical practice* (pp. 204–231). New York, NY: W. W. Norton.

Ogden, P. (2013). Technique and beyond: Therapeutic enactments, mindfulness, and the role of the body. In D. J. Siegel & M. Solomon (Eds.), *Healing moments in psychotherapy* (pp. 35–47). New York, NY: W. W. Norton.

Ogden, P., Minton, K., & Pain, C. (2006). *Trauma and the body: A sensorimotor approach to psychotherapy.* New York, NY: W. W. Norton.

Panksepp, J. (1998). *Affective neuroscience: The foundations of human and animal emotions.* New York, NY: Oxford University Press.

Panksepp, J. (2009). Brain emotional systems and qualities of mental life: From animal models of affect to implications for psychotherapeutics. In D. Fosha, D. J. Siegel, & M. Solomon (Eds.), *The healing power of emotion: Affective neuroscience, development, and clinical practice* (pp. 1–26). New York, NY: W. W. Norton.

Panksepp, J. (2012). *The archaeology of mind: Neuroevolutionary origins of human emotions.* New York, NY: W. W. Norton.

Porges, S. W. (2004). Neuroception: A subconscious system for detecting threat and safety. *Zero to Three: Bulletin of the National Center for Clinical Infant Programs, 24*(5), 19–24.

Porges, S. W. (2009). Reciprocal influences between body and brain in the perception and expression of affect: A polyvagal perspective. In D. Fosha, D. J. Siegel, & M. Solomon (Eds.), *The healing power of emotion: Affective neuroscience, development, and clinical practice* (pp. 27–54). New York, NY: W. W. Norton.

Porges, S. W. (2011). *The polyvagal theory: Neurophysiological foundations of emotions, attachment, communication, and self-regulation.* New York, NY: W. W. Norton.

Rizzolatti, G., & Craighero, L. (2004). The mirror-neuron system. *Annual Review of Neuroscience, 27*(1), 169–192.

Rose, N. R., & Abi-Rached, J. M. (2013). *Neuro: The new brain sciences and the management of the mind.* Princeton, NJ: Princeton University Press.

Schore, A. (2009). Right brain affect regulation: An essential mechanism of development, trauma, dissociation, and psychotherapy. In D. Fosha, D. J. Siegel, & M. Solomon (Eds.), *The healing power of emotion: Affective neuroscience, development, and clinical practice* (pp. 112–144). New York, NY: W. W. Norton.

Schore, A. (2011). Foreword. In P. Bromberg, *The shadow of the tsunami and the growth of the relational mind.* New York, NY: Routledge.

Schore, A. (2012). *The science of the art of psychotherapy.* New York, NY: W. W. Norton.

Shapiro, F. (2013). Redefining trauma and its hidden connections: Identifying and reprocessing the experiential contributors to a wide variety of disorders. In D. Fosha, D. J. Siegel, & M. Solomon (Eds.), *The healing power of emotion: Affective neuroscience, development, and clinical practice* (pp. 89–114). New York, NY: W. W. Norton.

Siegel, D. J. (2007). *The mindful brain.* New York, NY: W. W. Norton.

Siegel, D. J. (2010a). *The mindful therapist.* New York, NY: W. W. Norton.

Siegel, D. J. (2010b). *Mindsight.* New York, NY: Random House.

Siegel, D. J. (2012a). *The developing mind, second edition: How relationships and the brain interact to shape who we are.* New York, NY: Guilford Press.

Siegel, D. J. (2012b). *Pocket guide to interpersonal neurobiology: An integrative handbook of the mind.* New York, NY: W. W. Norton.

Siegel, D. J., & Bryson, T. P. (2011). *The whole-brain child: 12 Revolutionary strategies to nurture your child's developing mind.* New York, NY: Delacorte Press.

Siegel, D. J. (2017). *Mind: A journey to the heart of being human.* New York, NY: W. W. Norton.

Solomon, M., & Tatkin, S. (2011). *Love and war in intimate relationships: Connection, disconnection, and mutual regulation in couple therapy.* New York, NY: W. W. Norton.

Speca, M., Carlson, L. E., Goodey, E., & Angen, M. (2000). A randomized, wait-list controlled clinical trial: The effect of a mindfulness meditation-based stress reduction program on mood and symptoms of stress in cancer outpatients. *Psychosomatic Medicine, 62*(5), 613–622.

Suarez Pace, M. M., & Sandberg, J. G. (2012). Emotion and family therapy: Exploring female and male clinicians' attitudes about the use of emotion in therapy. *Journal of Systemic Therapies, 31*(1), 1–21.

Swan, A. H., & Scott, C. (2009). Complicated grief: Implications for the treatment of post-traumatic stress disorder in couples. *Sexual and Relationship Therapy, 24*(1), 16–29.

Teasdale, J. D., Segal, Z. V., Williams, J. M., Ridgeway, V. A., Soulsby, J. M., & Lau, M. A. (2000). Prevention of relapse/recurrence in major depression by mindfulness-based cognitive therapy. *Journal of Consulting and Clinical Psychology, 68*(4), 615–623.

Tomm, K. (1984). One perspective on the Milan systemic approach: Part II. Description of session format, interviewing style and interventions. *Journal of Marital and Family Therapy, 10*, 253–271.

Tronick, E. (2009). Multilevel meaning making and dyadic expansion of consciousness theory: The emotional and the polymorphic polysemic flow of meaning. In D. Fosha, D. J. Siegel, & M. Solomon (Eds.), *The healing power of emotion: Affective neuroscience, development, and clinical practice* (pp. 86–111). New York, NY: W. W. Norton.

Turner, V. (1969). *The ritual process: Structure and* anti-structure. Chicago, IL: Aldine.

van der Kolk, B. A. (2014). *The body keeps the score: Brain, mind, and body in the healing of trauma.* New York, NY: Viking Press.

Vygotsky, L. S. (1978). *Mind in society.* Cambridge, MA: Harvard University Press.

Vygotsky, L. S. (1986). *Thought and language.* A. Kozulin (Ed.). Cambridge, MA: MIT Press.

Watzlawick, P. (1984). *Invented reality: How do we know what we believe we know?* New York, NY: W. W. Norton.

White, M. (1986). Negative explanation, restraint and double description: A template for family therapy. *Family Process, 25*(2), 169–184.

White, M. (1988). The process of questioning: A therapy of literary merit. *Dulwich Centre Newsletter*, Winter, 8–14.

White, M. (1988/89). The externalizing of the problem and the re-authoring of lives and relationships. *Dulwich Centre Newsletter*, Summer, 5–28.

White, M. (2004). Working with people who are suffering the consequences of multiple trauma: A narrative perspective. *International Journal of Narrative Therapy and Community Work, 1*, 47–76.

White, M. (2005). Children, trauma and subordinate story development. *International Journal of Narrative Therapy and Community Work, 3/4*, 10–21.

White, M. (2007). *Maps of narrative practice.* New York, NY: W. W. Norton.

White, M. (2011). *Narrative practice: Continuing the conversations.* New York, NY: W. W. Norton.

White, M., & Epston, D. (1990). *Narrative means to therapeutic ends.* New York, NY: W. W. Norton.

Wilder, E. J. (2004). *The complete guide to living with men.* Lexington, KY: Shepherd's House.

Wilkinson, M. (2010). *Changing minds in therapy: Emotion, attachment, trauma, and neurobiology.* New York, NY: W. W. Norton.

Zimmerman, J. L. (2017). Neuro-narrative therapy: Brain Science, Narrative

Therapy, Poststructuralism, and Preferred Identities. *Journal of Systemic Therapies, 36*(2), 12–26.

Zimmerman, J. L., & Beaudoin, M. N. (2015). Neurobiology for your narrative: How brain science can influence narrative work. *Journal of Systemic Therapies, 34*(2), 56–71.

Zimmerman, J. L., & Dickerson, V. G. (1996). *If problems talked: Narrative therapy in action.* New York, NY: Guilford Press.

Index

Abi-Rached, J.M., 2, 9, 18, 186
accountability
  of therapist, 184–85
acting out
  SNS arousal in, 149
action
  bodily responses as precursors
    to, 92
actualization
  development of highest levels of, 8
adaptive information processing
  of experience, 139, 140
adaptive process
  described, 138
addiction(s)
  opiate, 40
affect, 29–71
  from brain science perspective,
    36–38
  defined, 22, 45
  described, 179–80
  dysregulated, 162–68
  implicit, 160–61
  importance of, 22–24, 36–38
  in influencing identities, 27–28
  internalization of, 48, 67
  intolerable, 162
  lack of, 50
  in narratives, 20

  in narrative therapy, 29–71
  negative, 44
  negative over positive, 60
  in neuro-narrative therapy,
    179–80
  neuroscience in, 1–2
  regulation of, 148–57
  scaffolding, 68
affective decision making
  dissociation in prevention of,
    153
affective experience(s)
  linked to problem-influenced
    MOMENTS, 54
  right brain in creating, 111–14
  tracking fluctuations of felt sense
    of, 87
affective mentality
  over cognitive functions, 37
affective neuroscience
  implications for privileging emo-
    tions and, 23
affect management
  narrative therapy in facilitating,
    182–84
  therapeutic relationship in facili-
    tating, 183–84
affect regulation, 148–57
  in attachment, 105

development(s)
  as examples of resistance, 34
developmental trauma
  effects of, 160
dharma, 82
*Diagnostic and Statistical Manual of
  Mental Disorders* (DSM)
  on internalizing problems, 10
disconnection
  from feelings, 60
discourse(s)
  internalized, 11
  internalizing *vs.* externalizing,
    10–11
  problems with terminology of, 9
discussion(s)
  problem-related, 48
dissociation, 149, 150
  in affective decision making pre-
    vention, 153
  described, 152
  effects of, 152–53
  as perceptual phenomenon, 153
  in problem MOMENTS, 153
  separation of mental processes in,
    152–53
distress
  mirror neurons in signaling, 158
  separation, 39–40
divided attention, 138
dominance displays
  reasons for, 118
"double-listening," 52
drive(s)
  nonconscious, 22–23
DSM. *see Diagnostic and Statistical Manual of Mental Disorders*
  (DSM)
Dulwich International Narrative
  conference, xiii
Dylan, B., xiii

dysregulated affect, 163
  identities and, 162–68
dysregulation
  described, 162–63

Ecker, B., 140, 141
EEG studies. *see* electrocardiography
  (EEG) studies
electrocardiography (EEG) studies
  of right-brain to right-brain com-
    munication, 114
embodiment
  lack of, 23–24
embodying, 73–100
EMDR. *see* eye movement desensitization and reprocessing (EMDR)
emotion(s), 29–71
  in activating memories, 135
  arousal and story related to, 38,
    43–46
  bodily experiences of, 74
  defined, 22, 45
  described, 45
  as facilitating, 37
  in family therapy literature, 6
  as focal organizer of brain func-
    tions, xii
  impact on interpretations, 104
  implicitly avoiding, 23–24
  importance in therapy, 67
  in narrative therapy, 22–24,
    29–71
  negative *see* negative emotions
  in neuro-narrative therapy, xiv
  nonconscious, 22–23
  positive. *see* positive emotions
  privileging, 23
  remember, 70
  role in MFT, 3–4
  shared, 20
  vulnerable, 123

moment-to-moment processing
of experiences of positive change, 61
moment-to-moment relational experience, 120–22
mPFC. see middle prefrontal cortex (mPFC)
MRT. see memory reconsolidation therapy (MRT)
multiple identities
meanings of, 165
multiple selves
idea of, 132
Myerhoff, B., 21

"name it to tame it," 48
narrative(s)
affect in, 20
components of, 169–70
left- and right-hemisphere modes of processing in, 19
makeup of, 19–20
mental experiences missing from, 19
in narrative therapy, 119–23
new, 169–70
problem-supporting, 20
as right-brain functions, 19–20
narrative construction
historical reflection vs., 112
narrative frame
expansion of, 169–70
narrative ideas and practices
integration with, 15
narrative IPNB style, 18–21
narrative literature
unique outcomes in, 34
narrative meaning, 119–20
narrative metaphor
in narrative therapy, 21
narrative psychotherapy
mindfulness meditation with, 83–84

narrative questions
UOMs–related, 64, 147
narrative self
defined, 14
minimum self vs., 14
narrative therapist(s)
described, 179
from family therapists to, 3
history of, 7–8
suspicious of scientific knowledge, 7–9
unique outcome questions by, 147
narrative therapy
affect in, 29–71. see also affect
background of, 6
bodily based ideas in, 87–95
body/mindfulness practices in, 73–100. see also body/mindfulness practices
with children, 75
cognitive influence of, 37
critical questions pertinent to integration of neuro with, 177–90
described, 27
dual landscape in, 7
EMDR in, 139–40, 142
emotional systems in, 37
emotions in, 22–24, 29–71, 67
in facilitating affect management, 182–84
focus of, 36, 182
giving meaning to experience in, 77
history of, 1–12
idea of multiple identities or versions of self in, 132
introduction, xiii–xv
meaning making in, 6–7
minds in, 77–81
narrative metaphor in, 21
nonconscious influences in, 129–75. see also nonconscious influences